I am grateful to God for all the things he has done. I dedicate this book to him
and to my family who have always believed in me.
Thank you for everything.

Jonatas Rodrigues
2024

This Book Belongs to:

○————————————————————————————————————○

Test Color Page

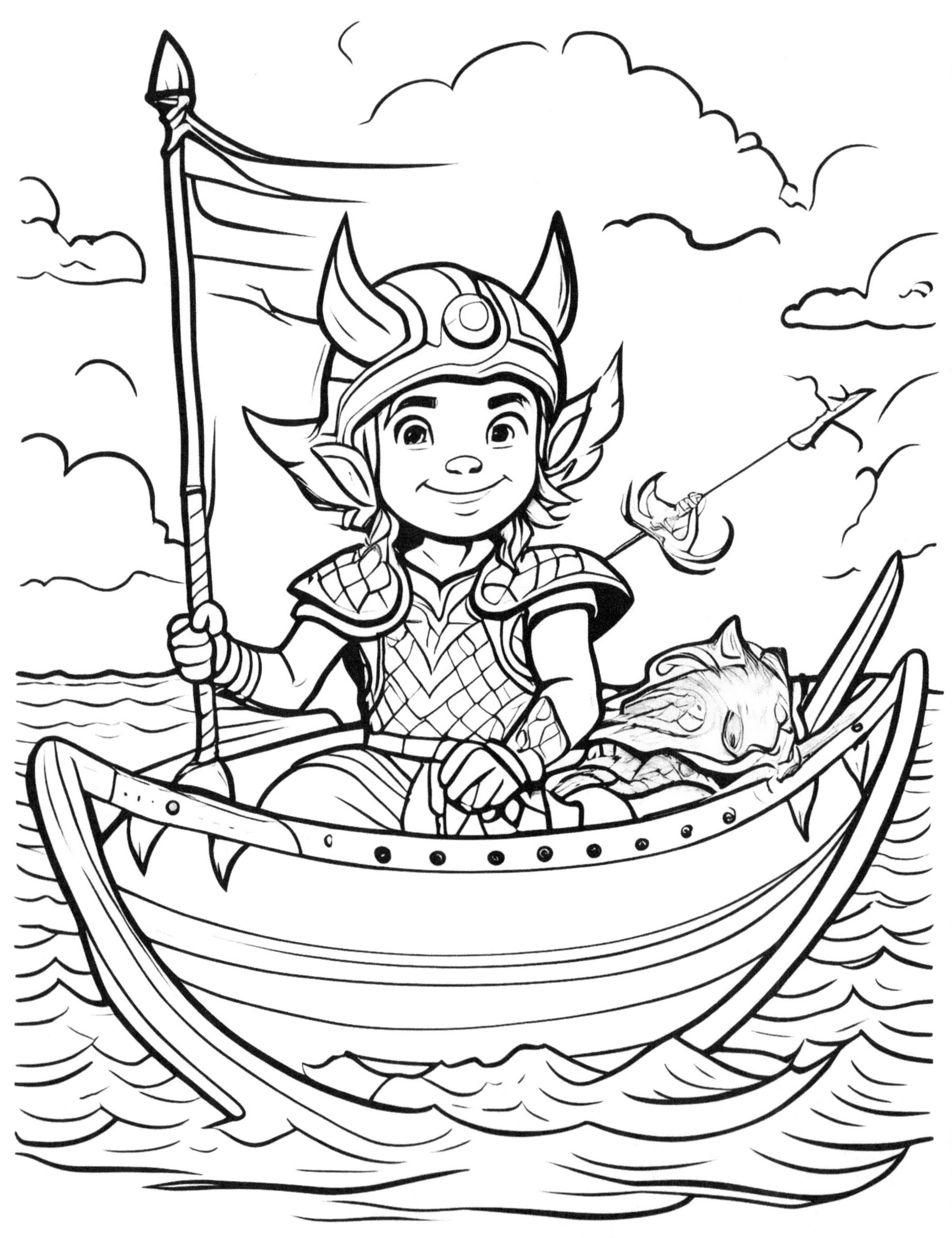

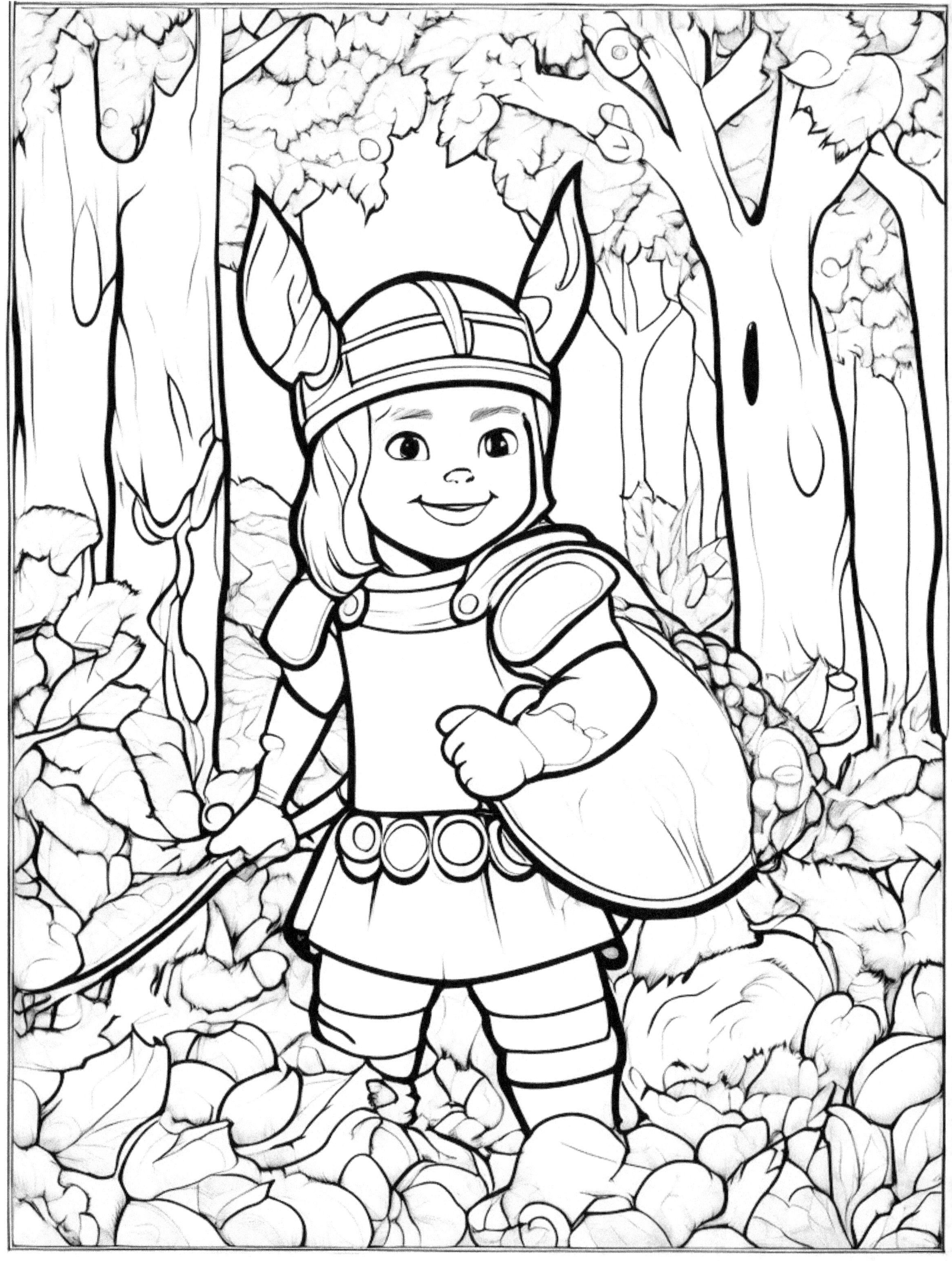

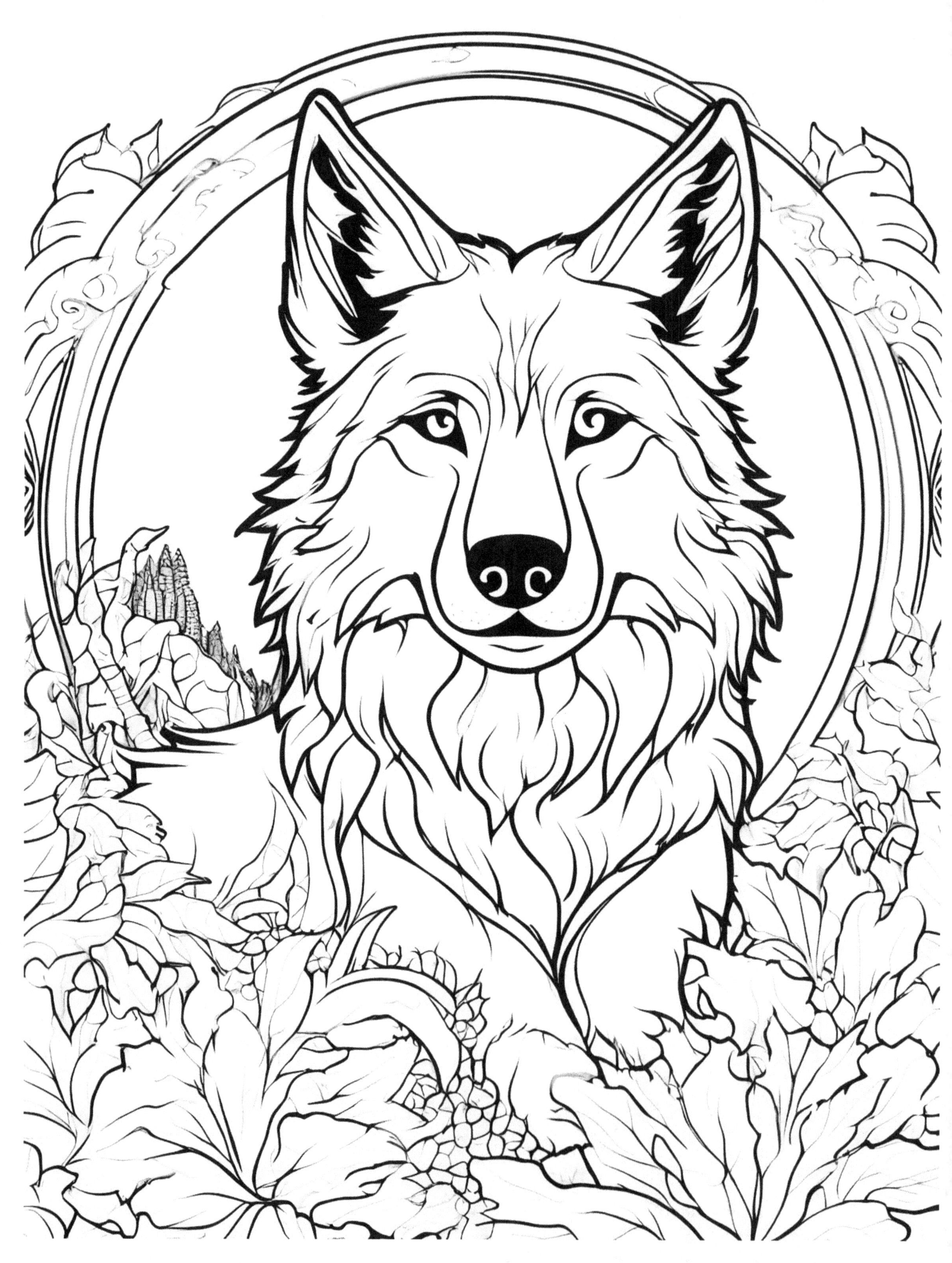

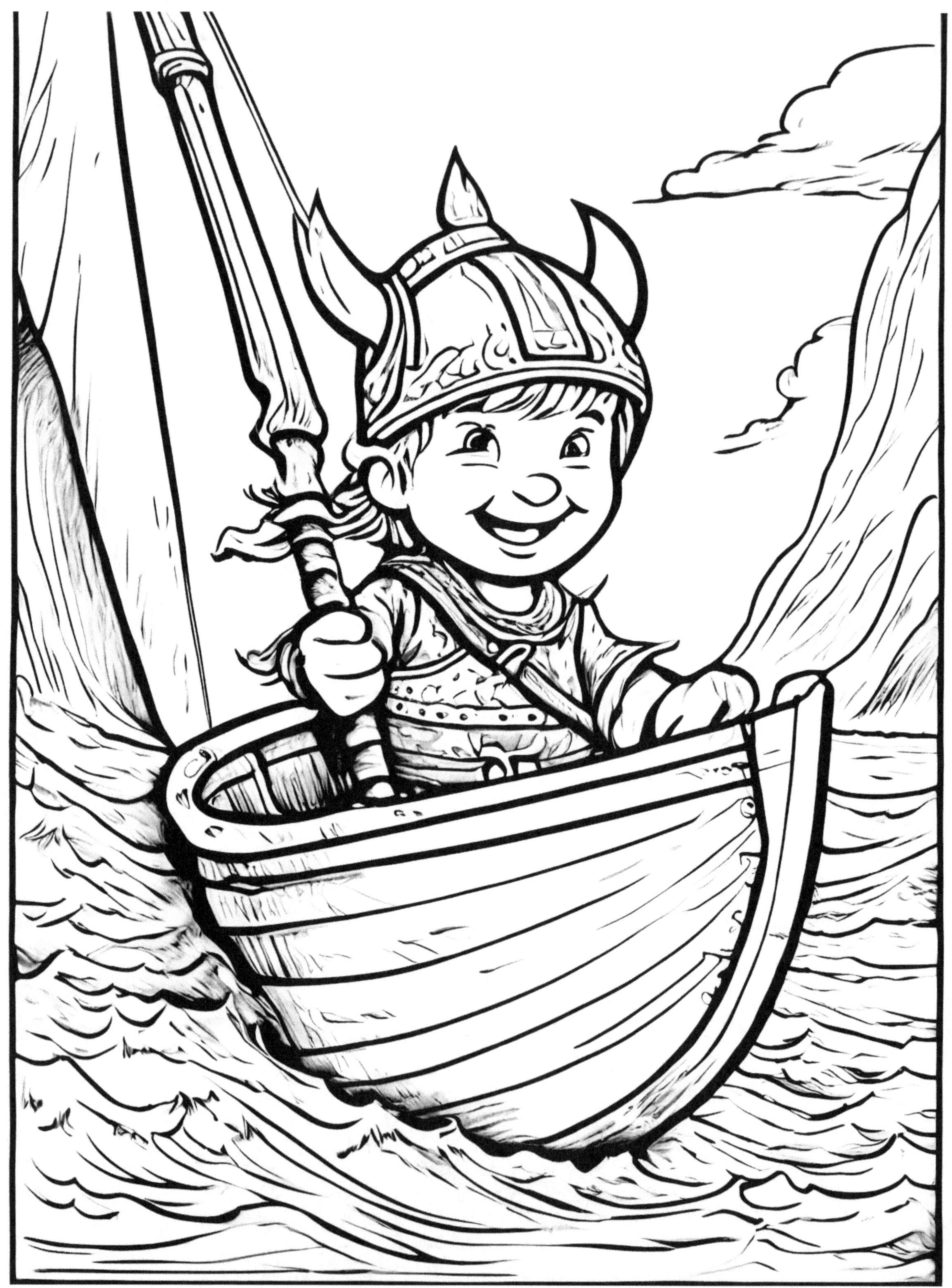

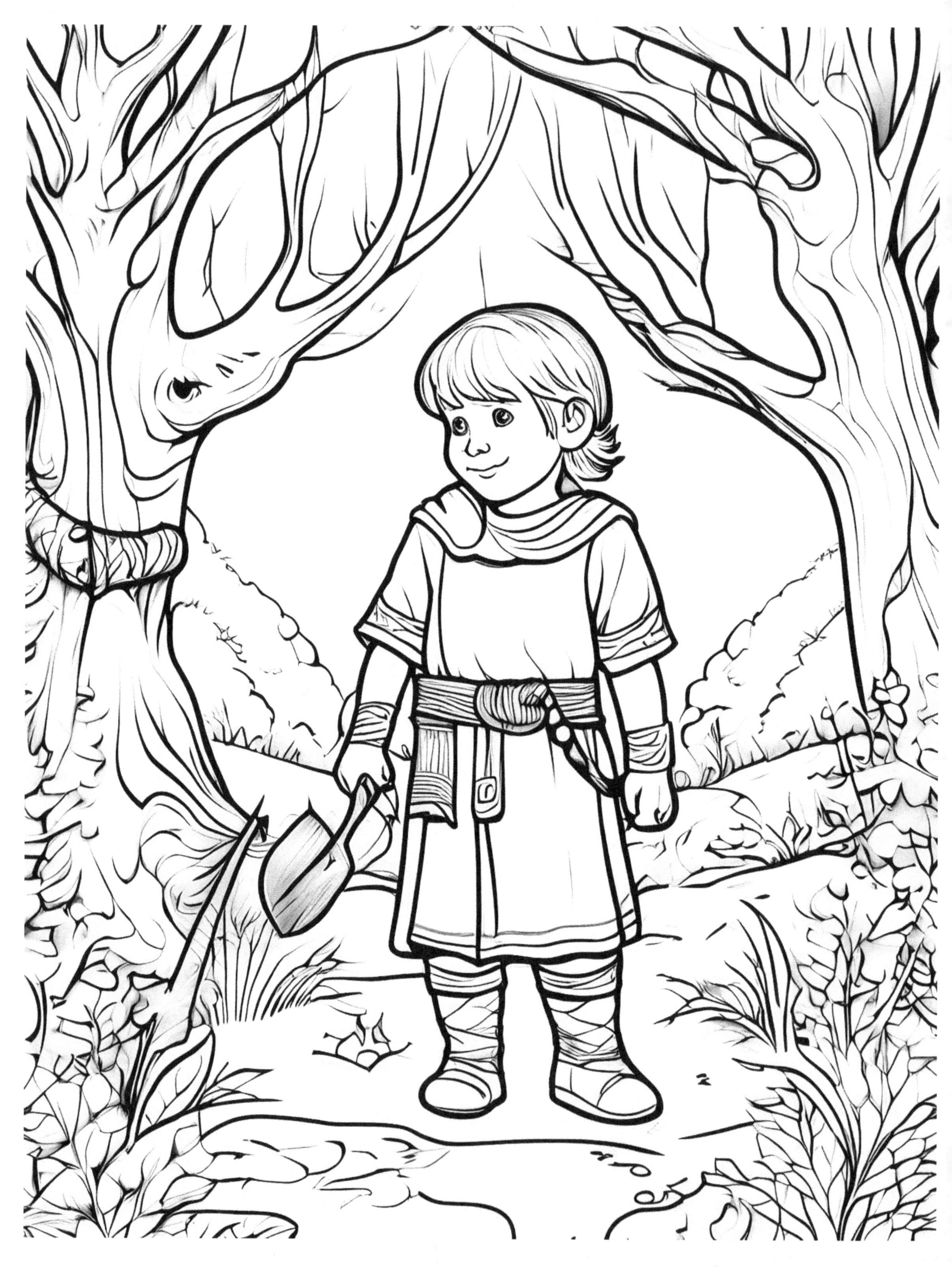

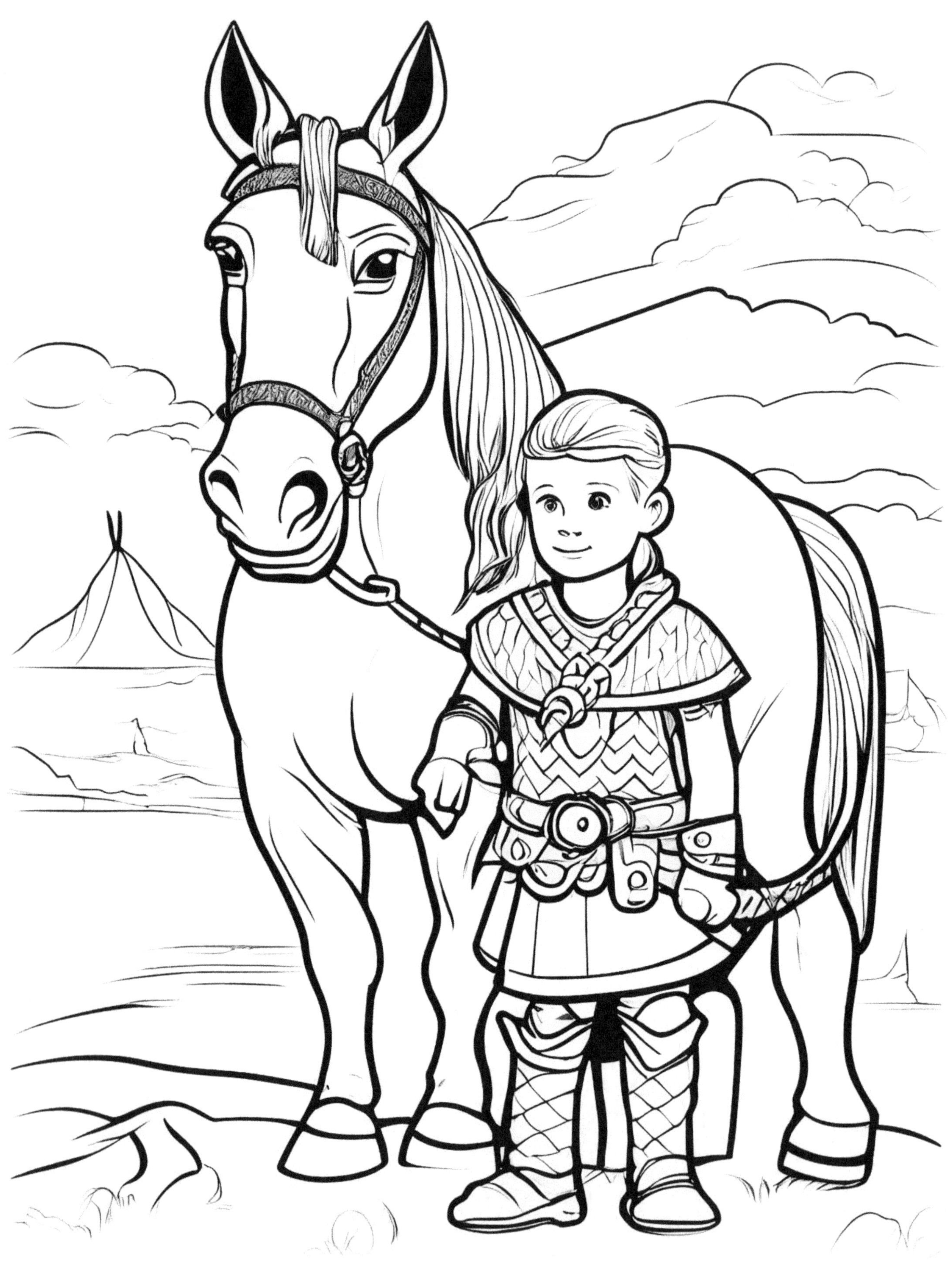

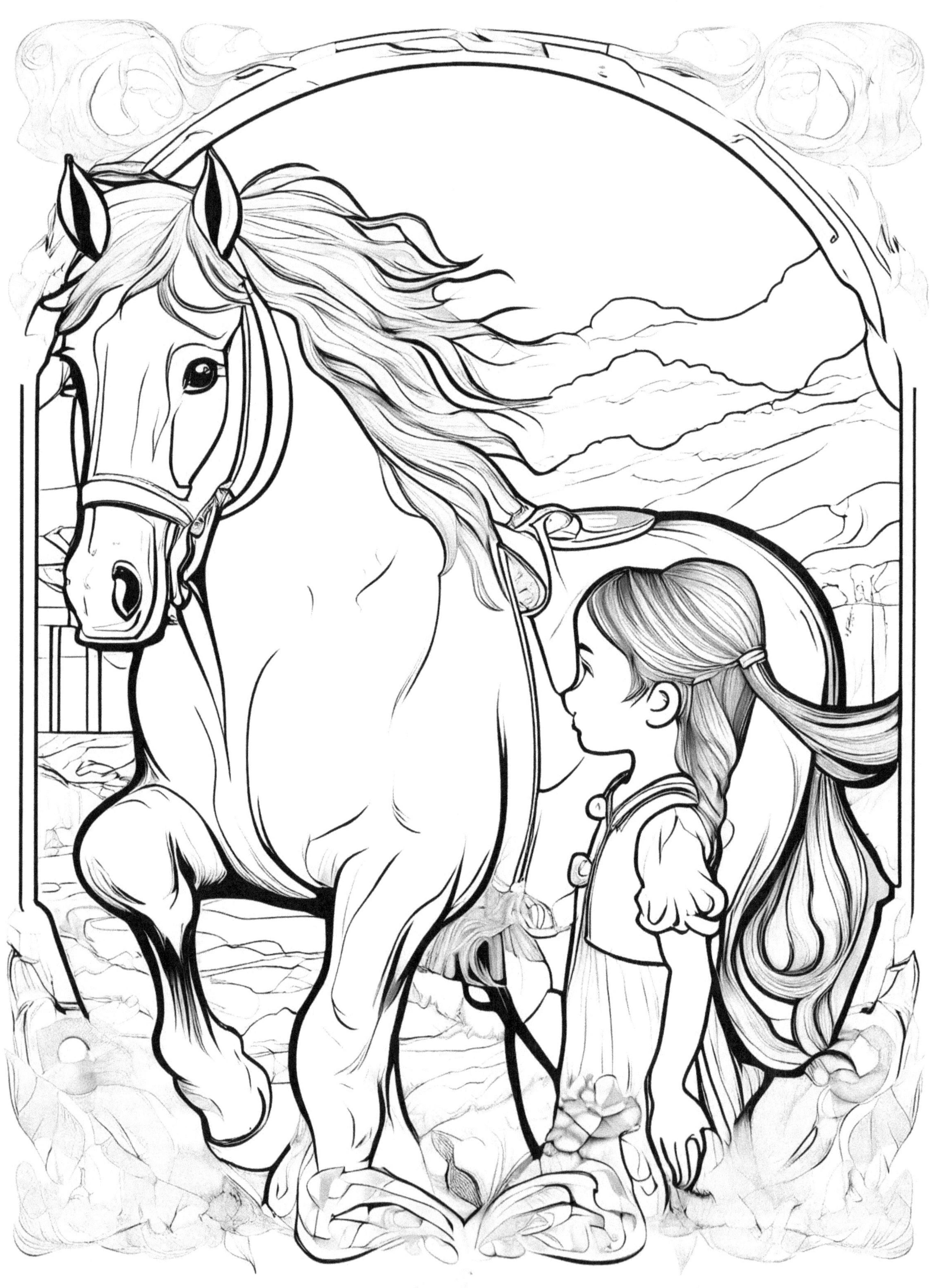

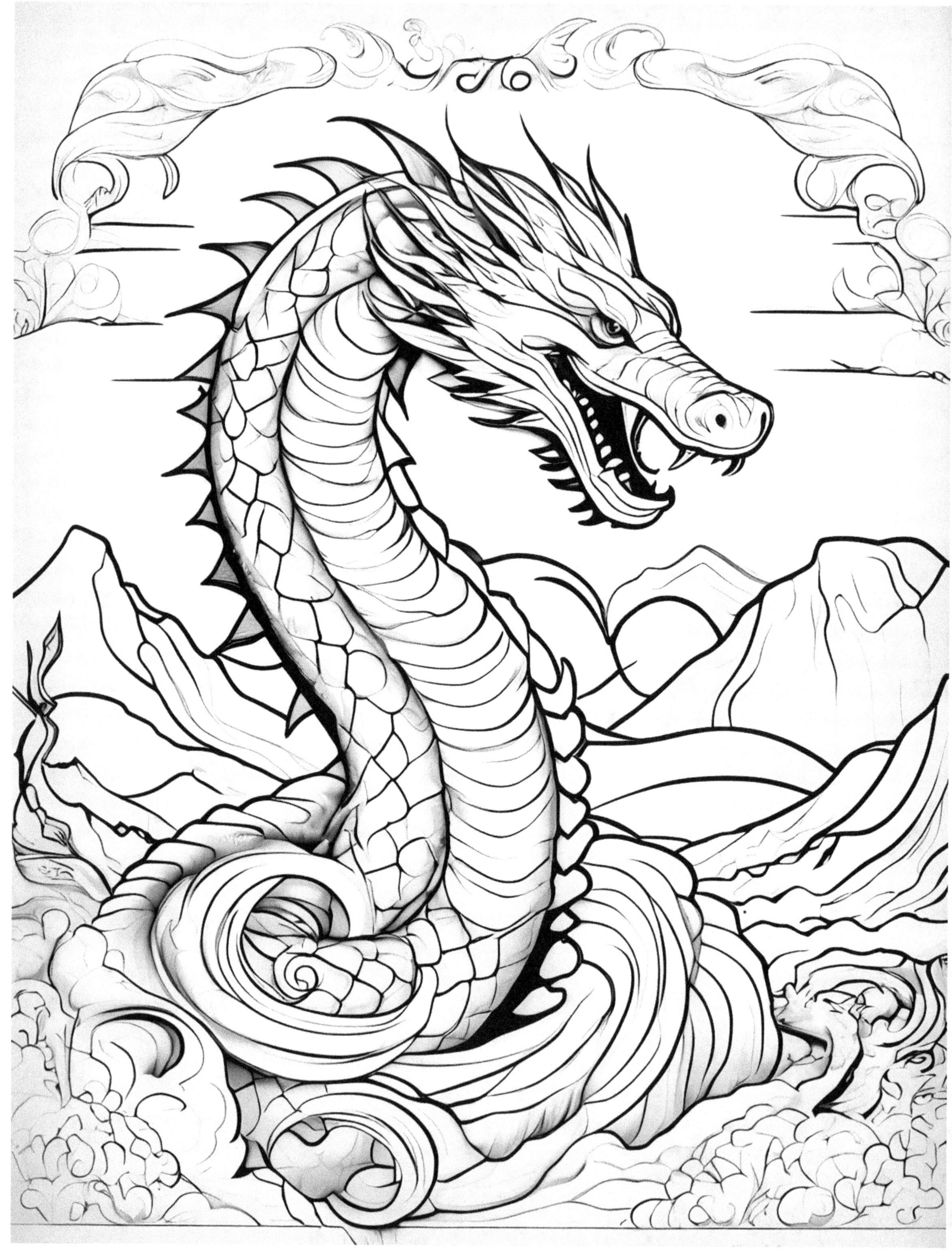

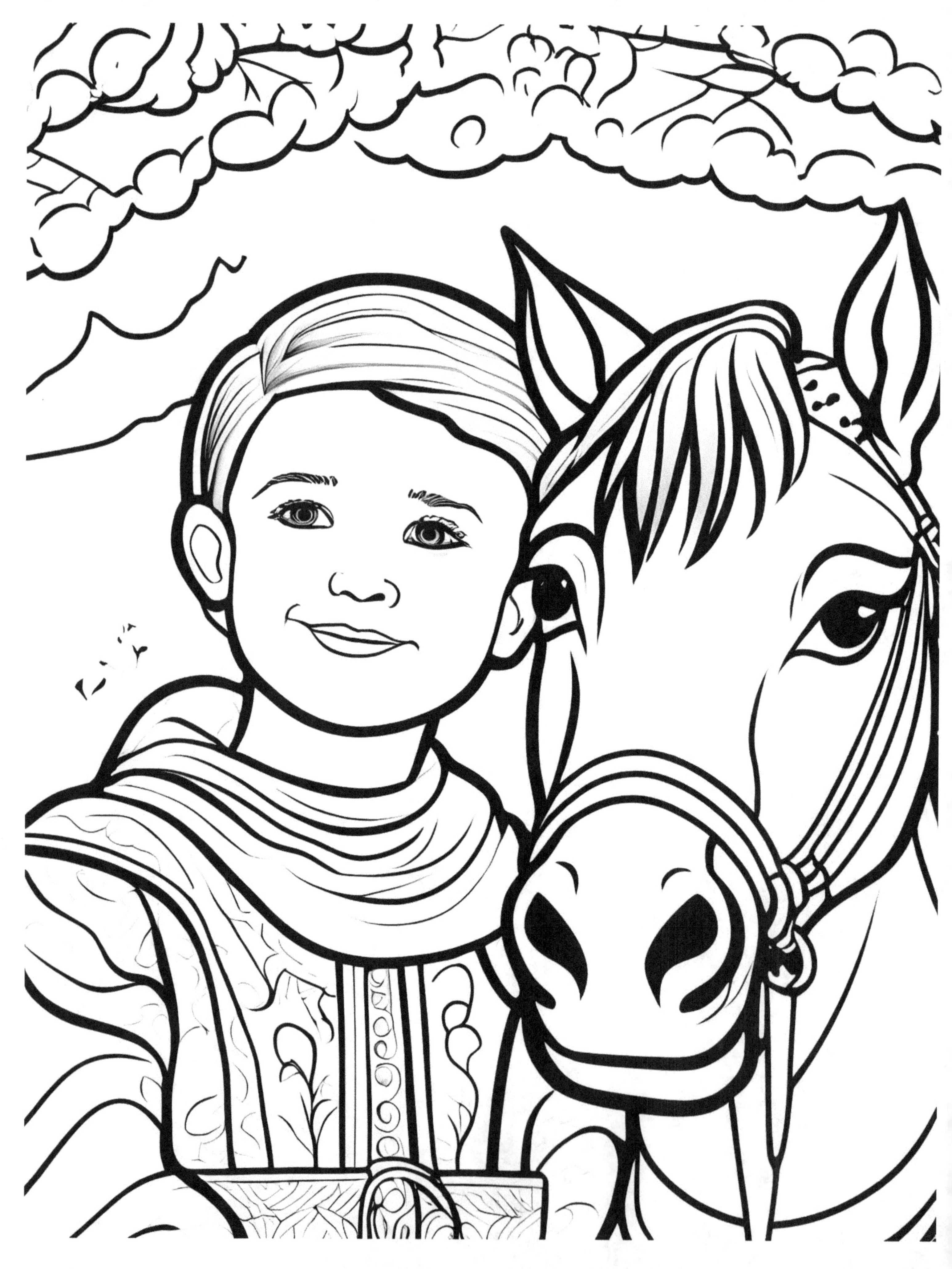

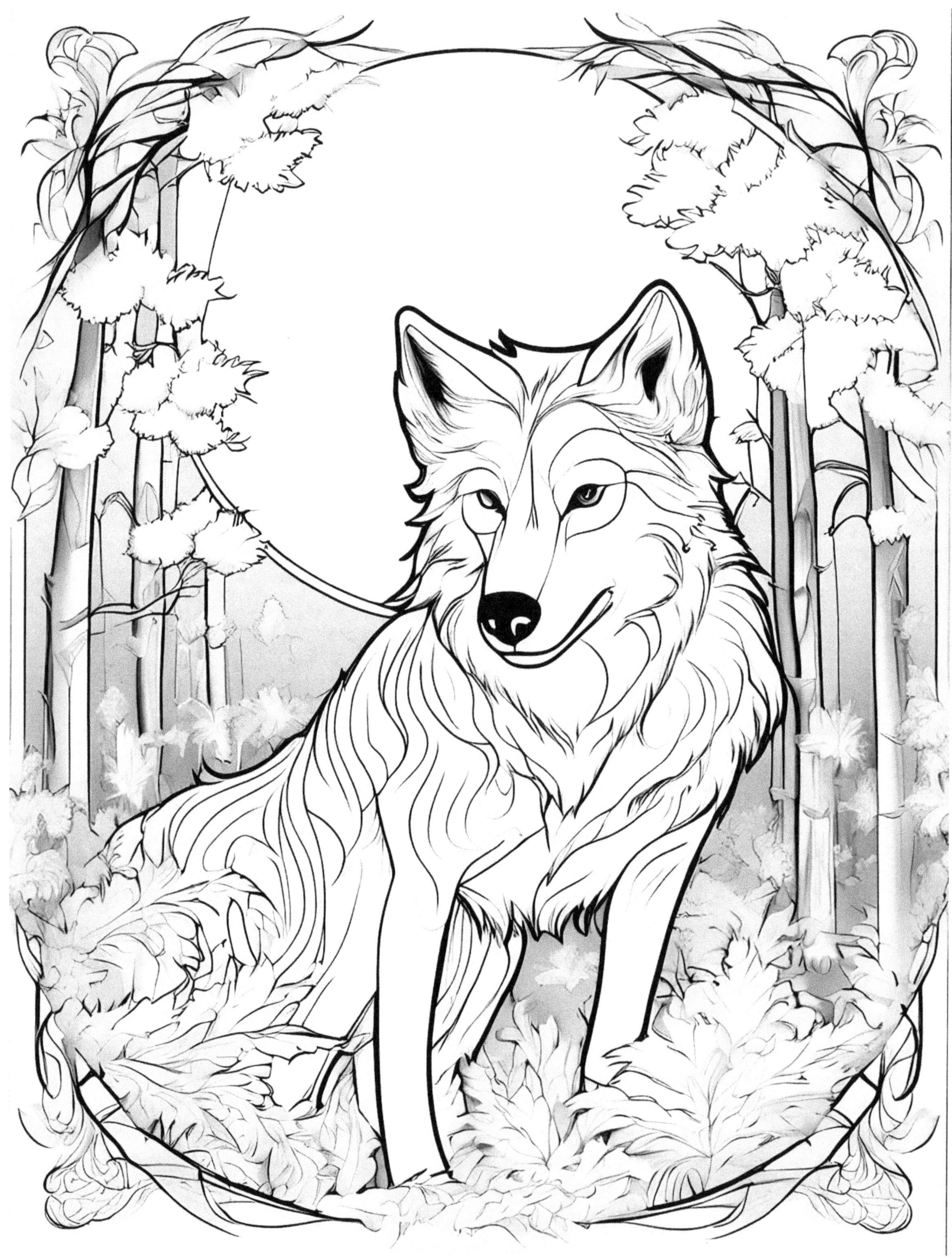

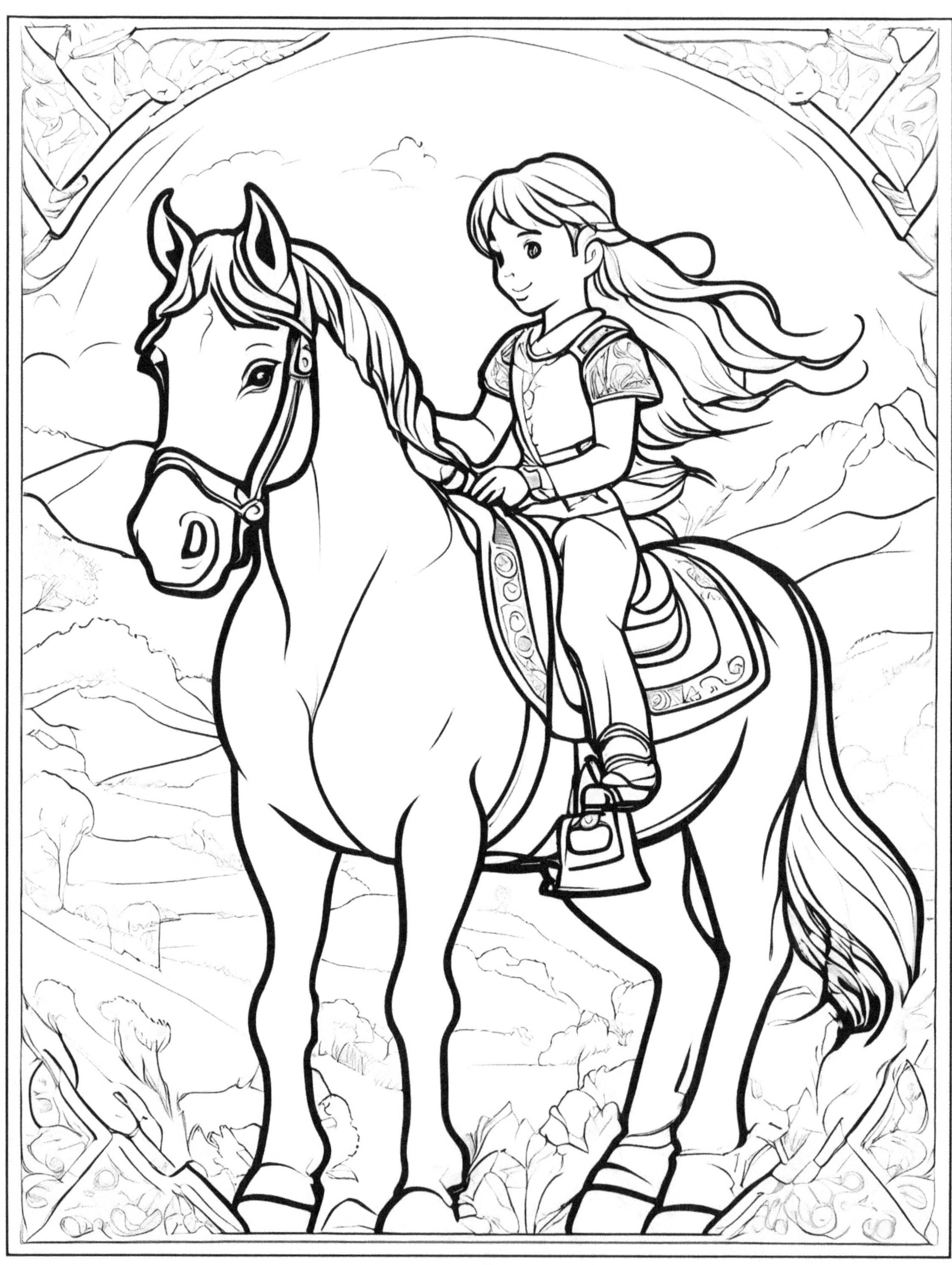

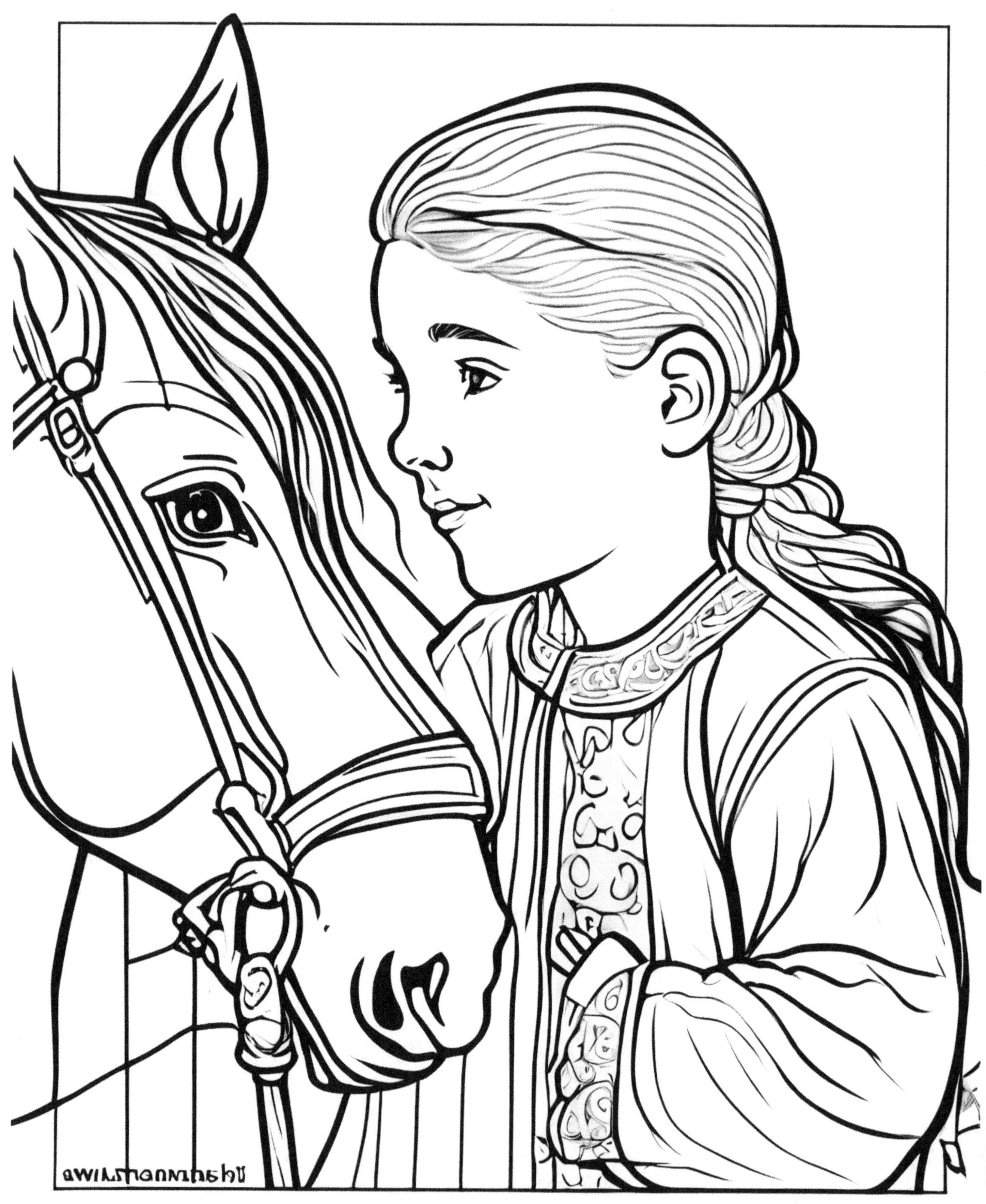

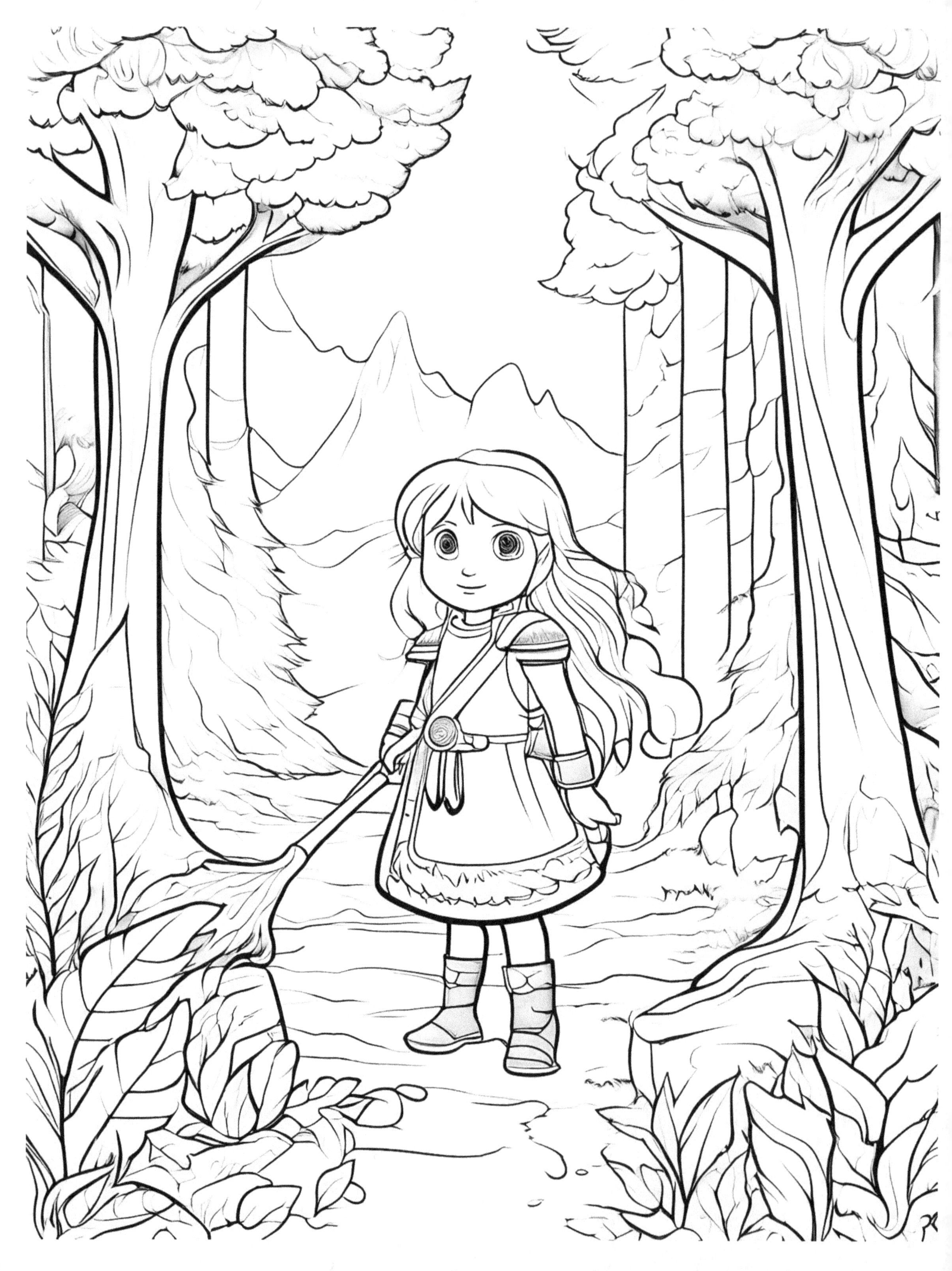

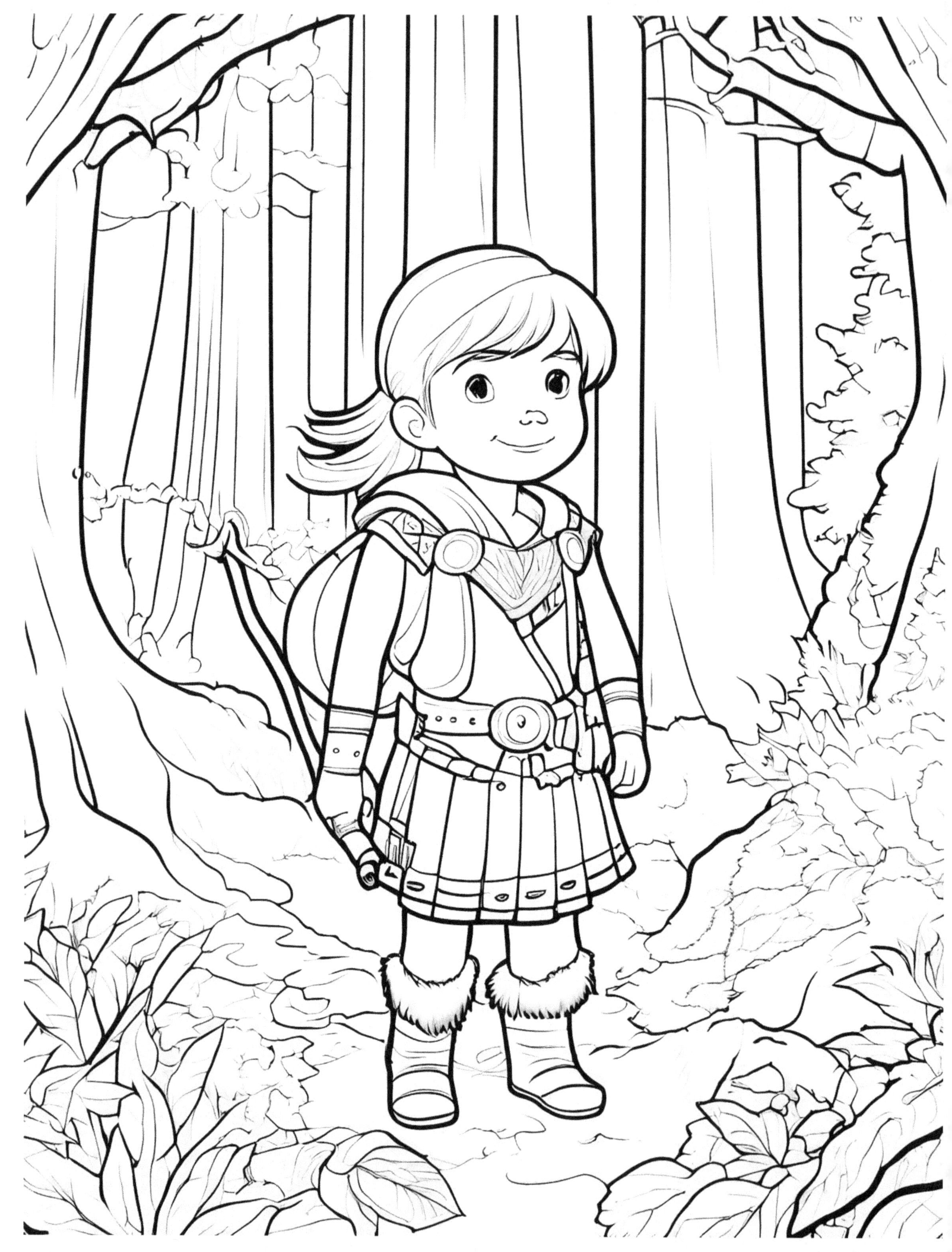

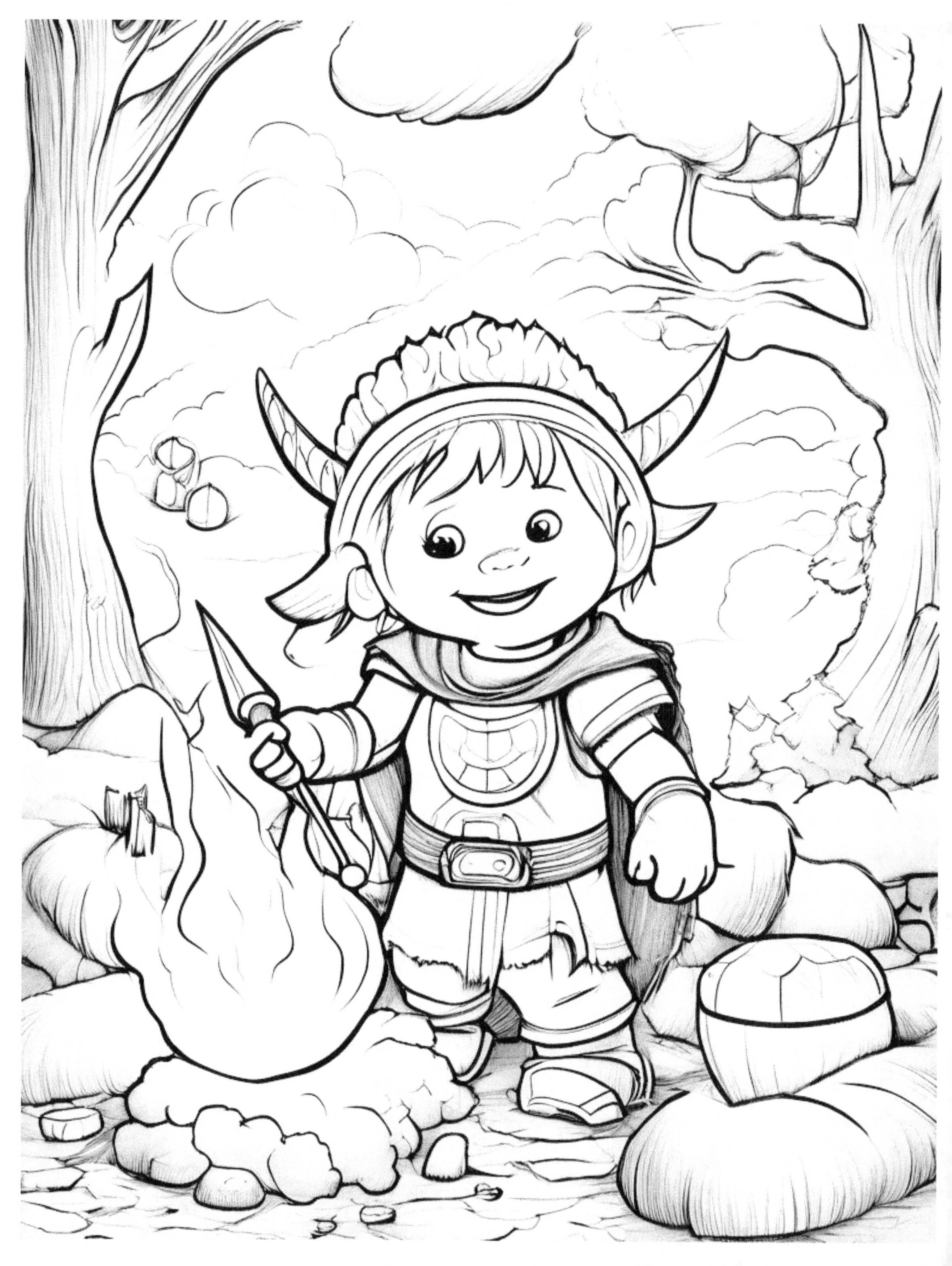

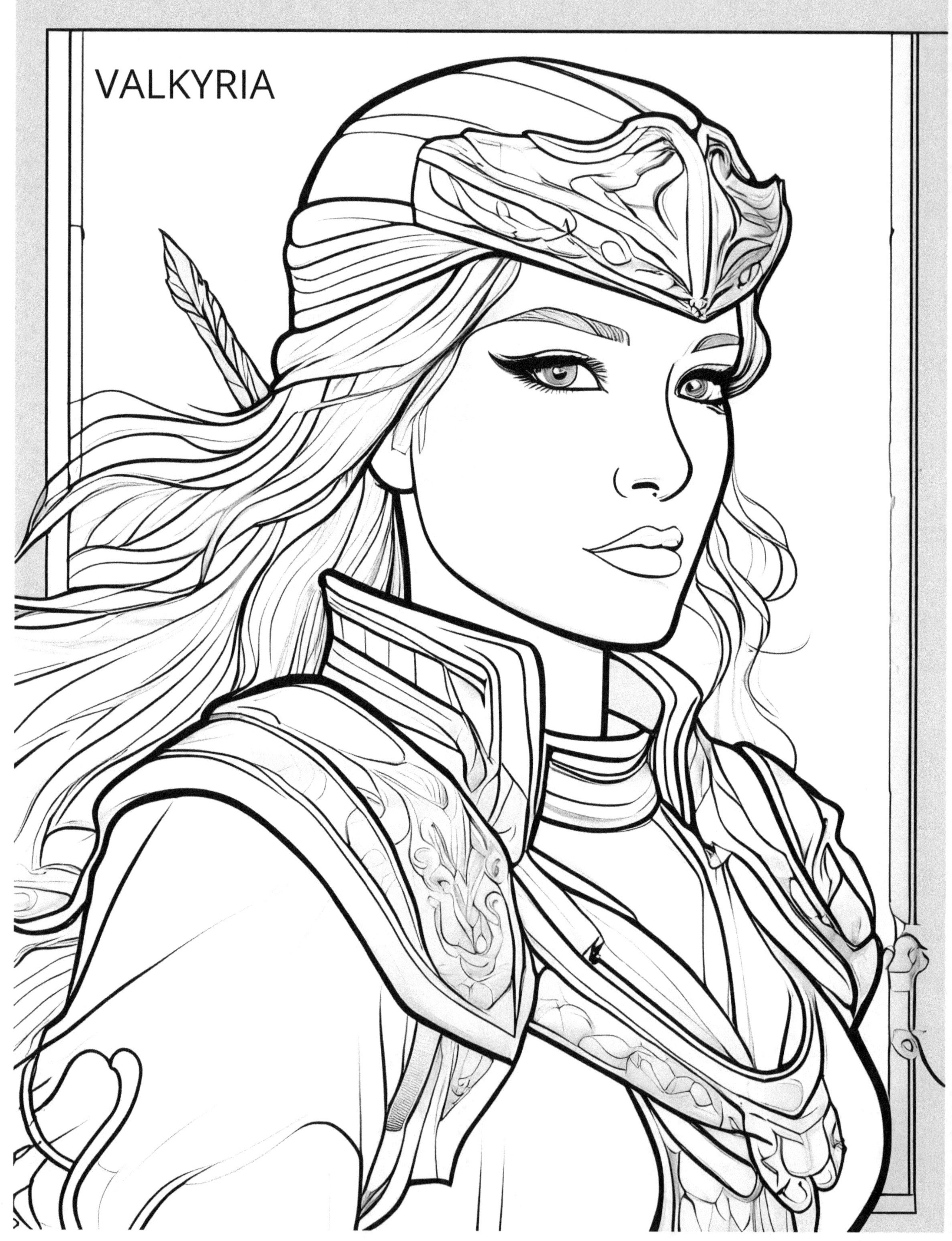
VALKYRIA

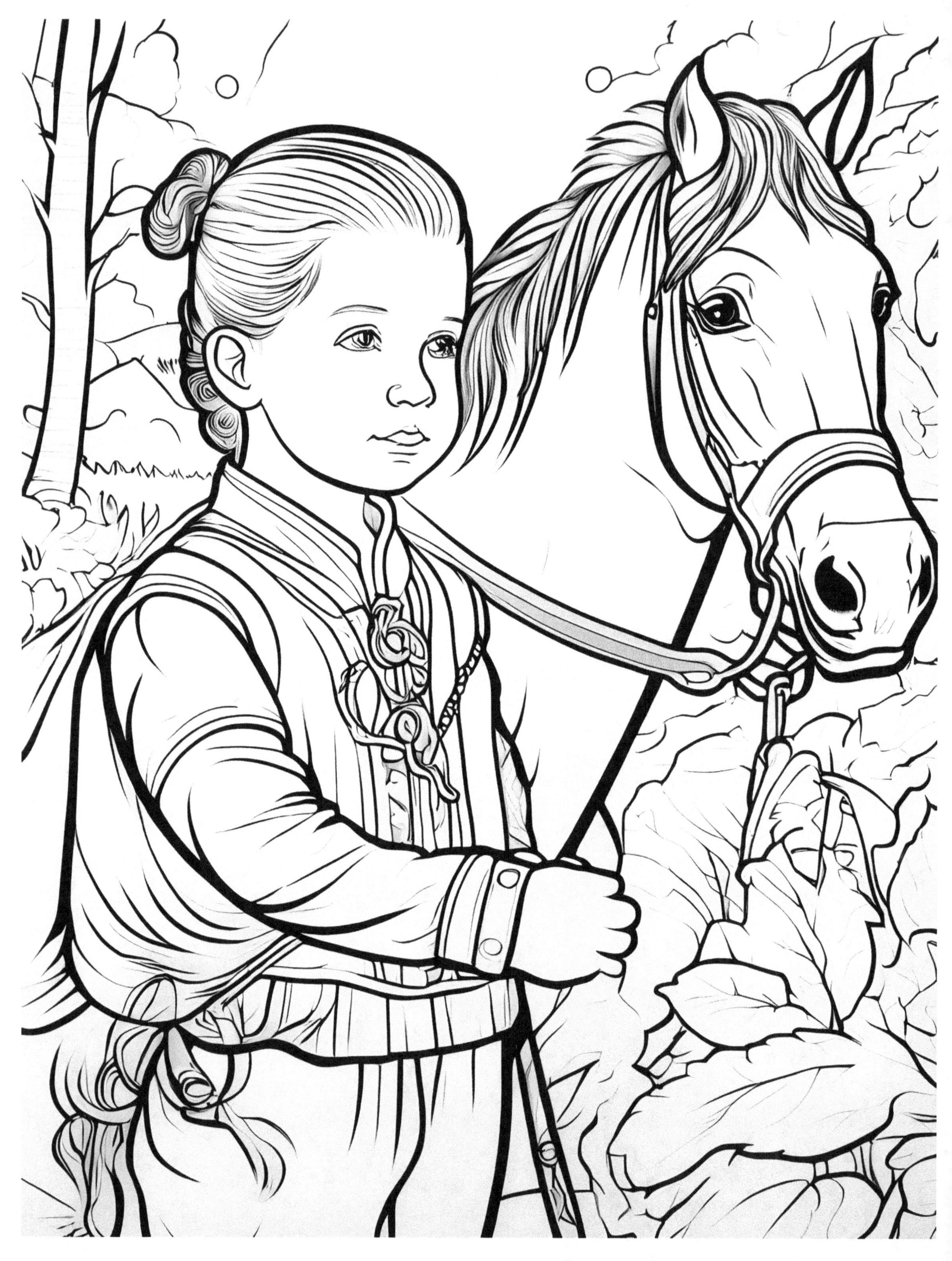

FREYA

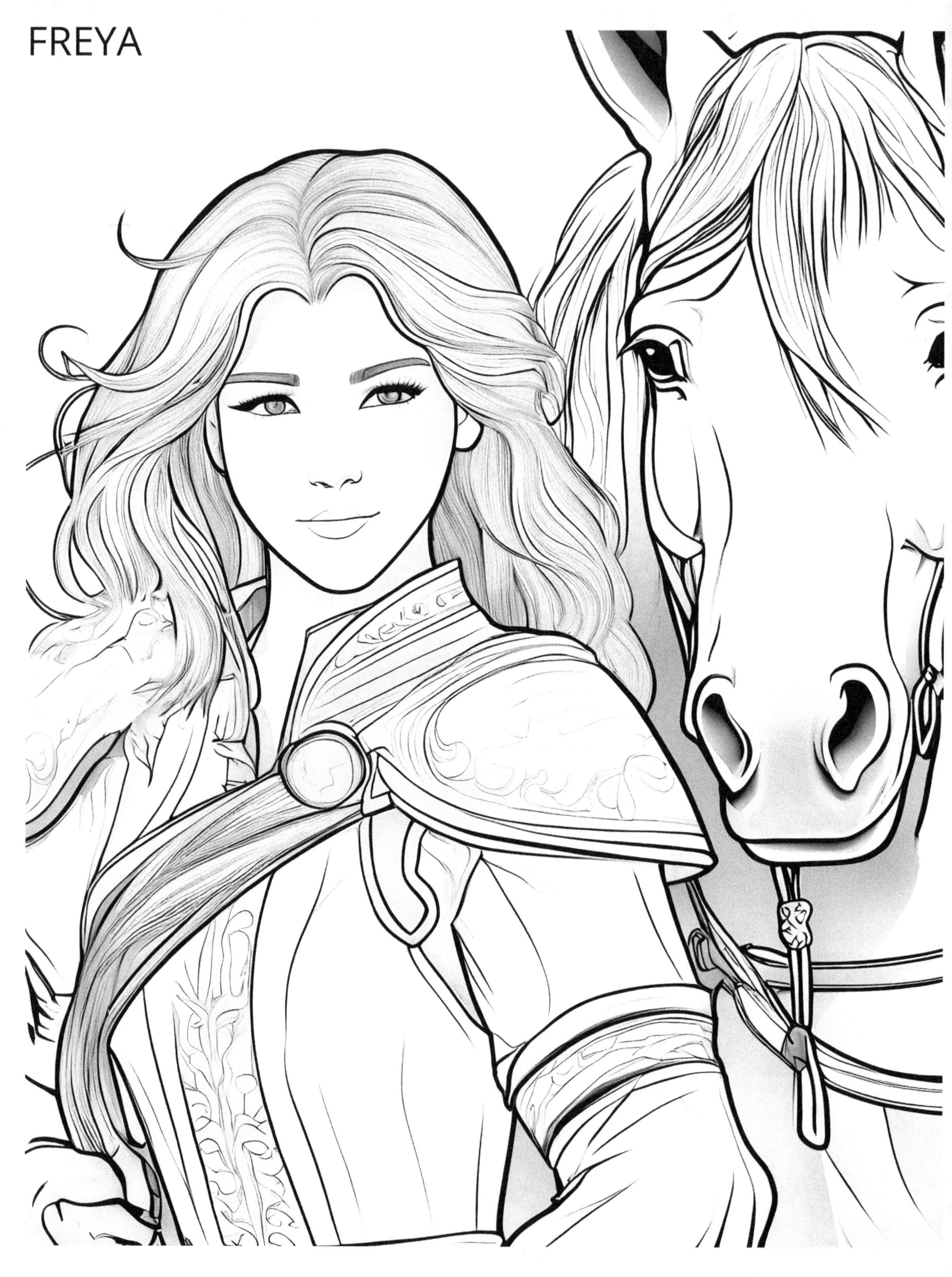

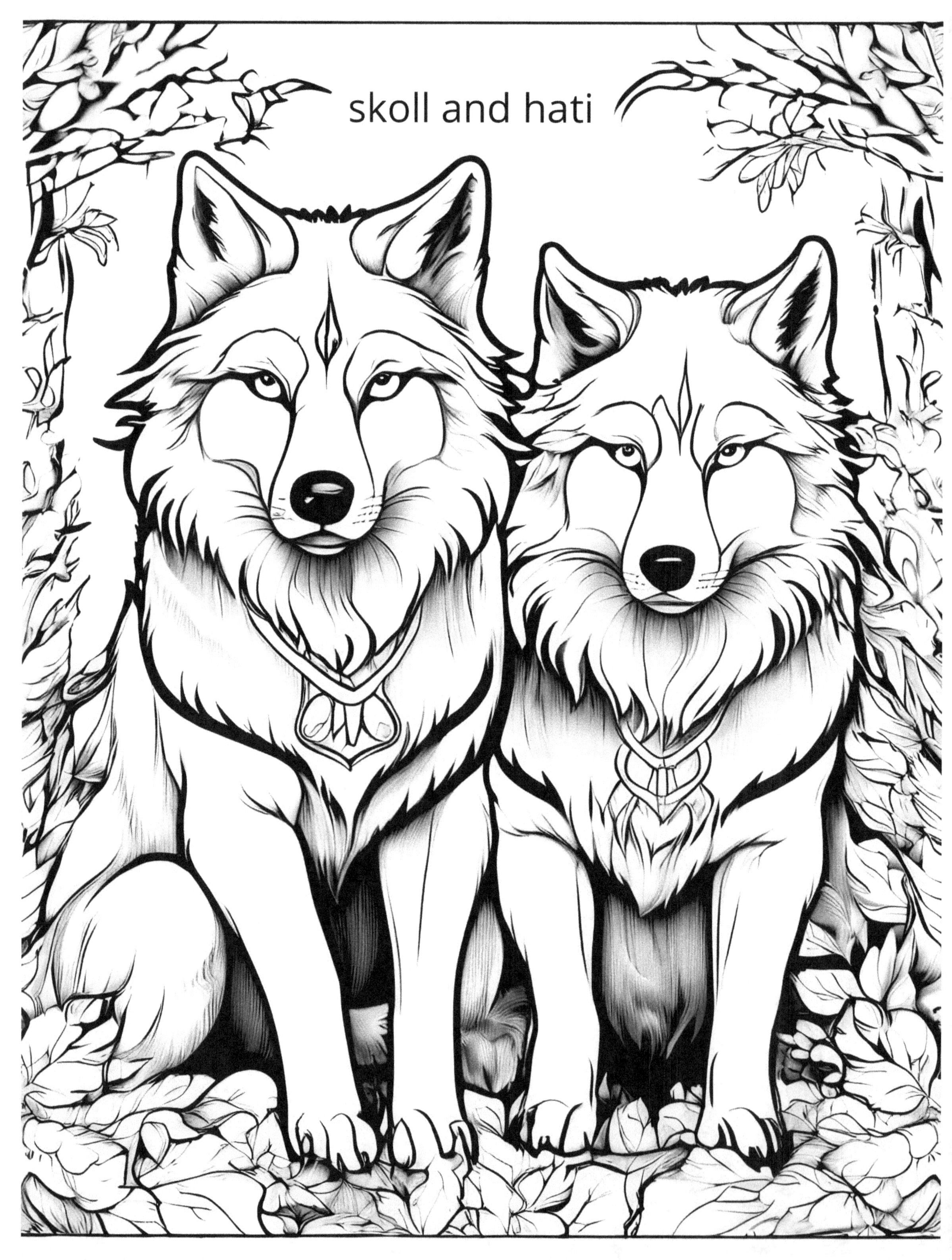

skoll and hati

FENRIR

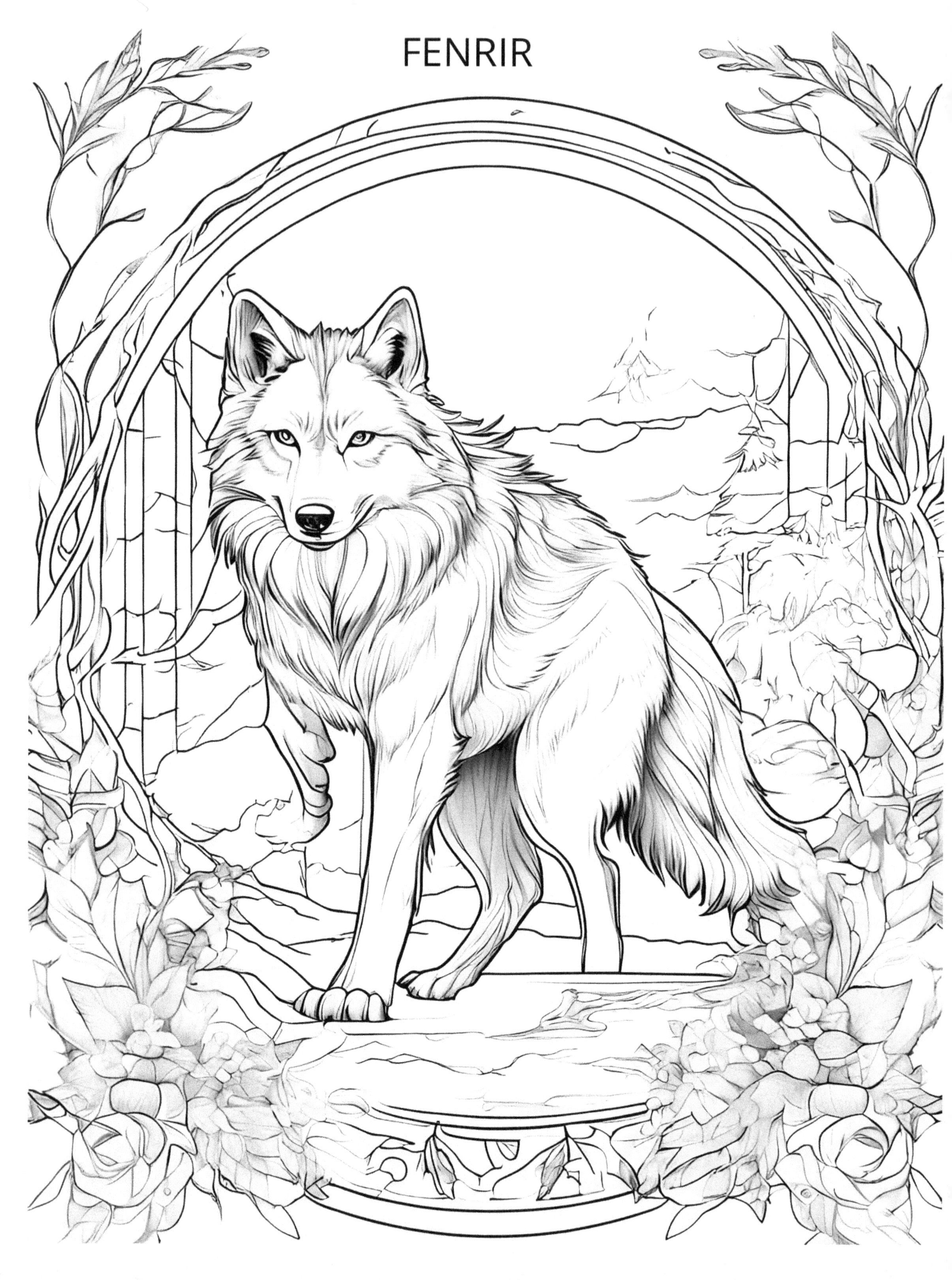

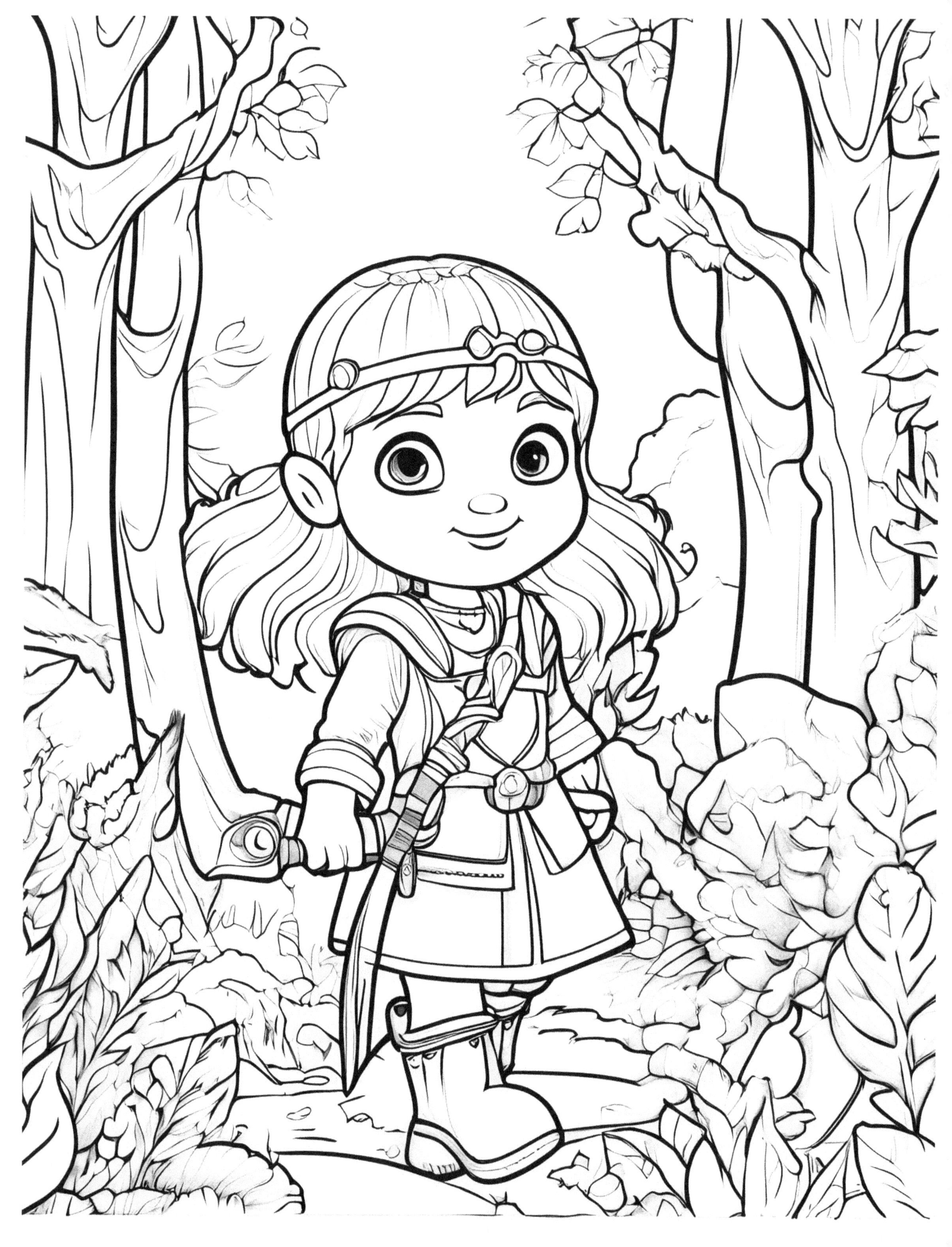

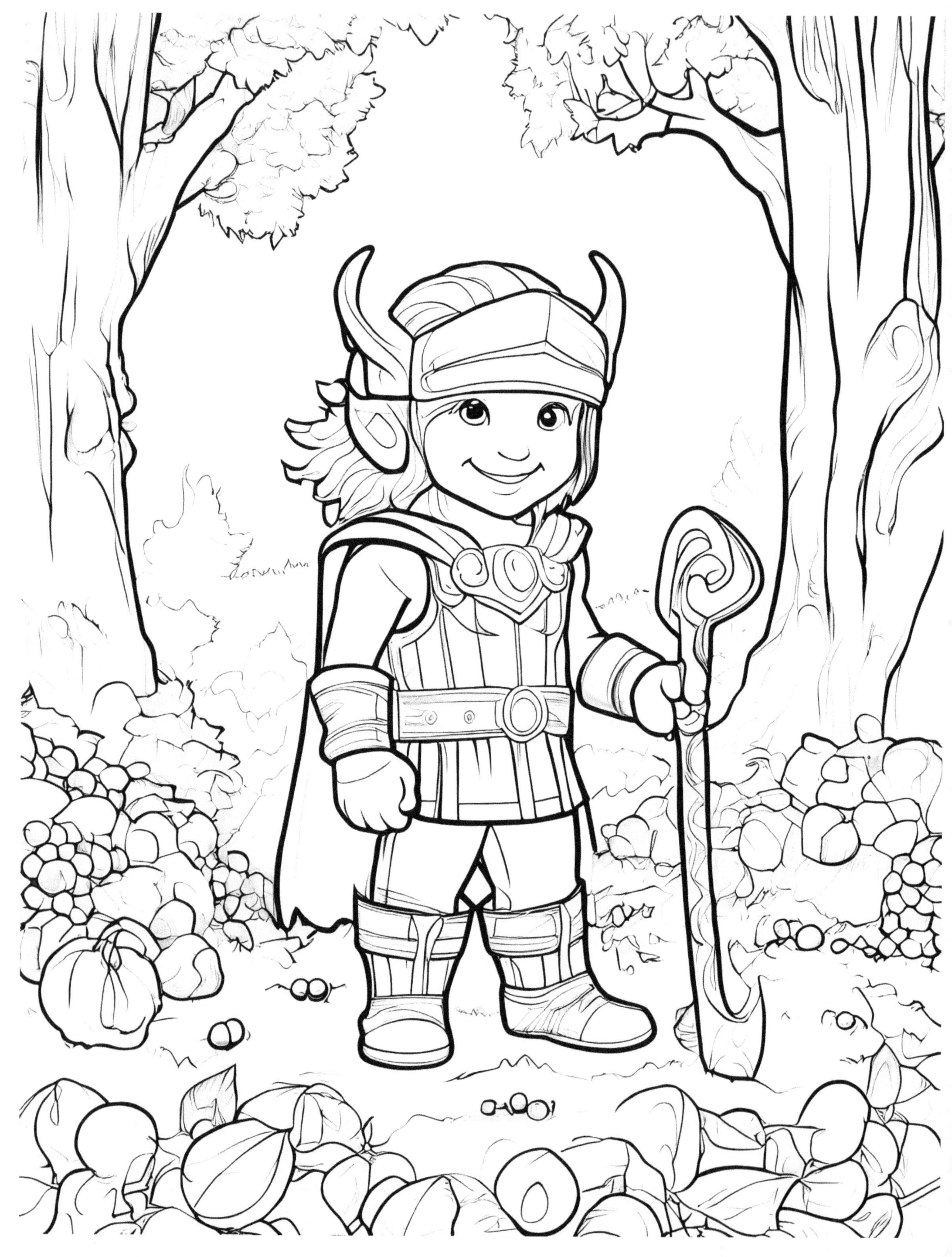

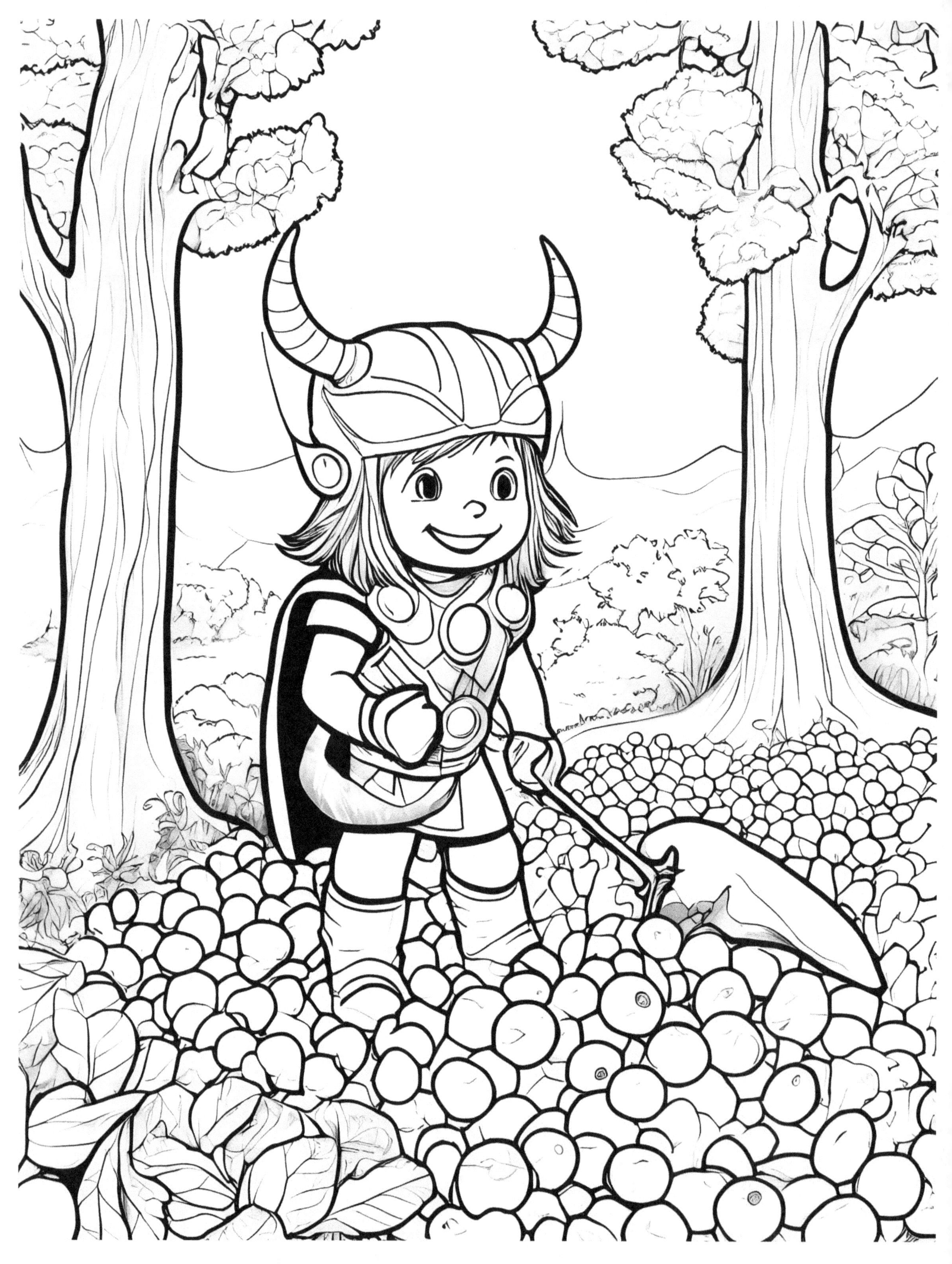

ODIN

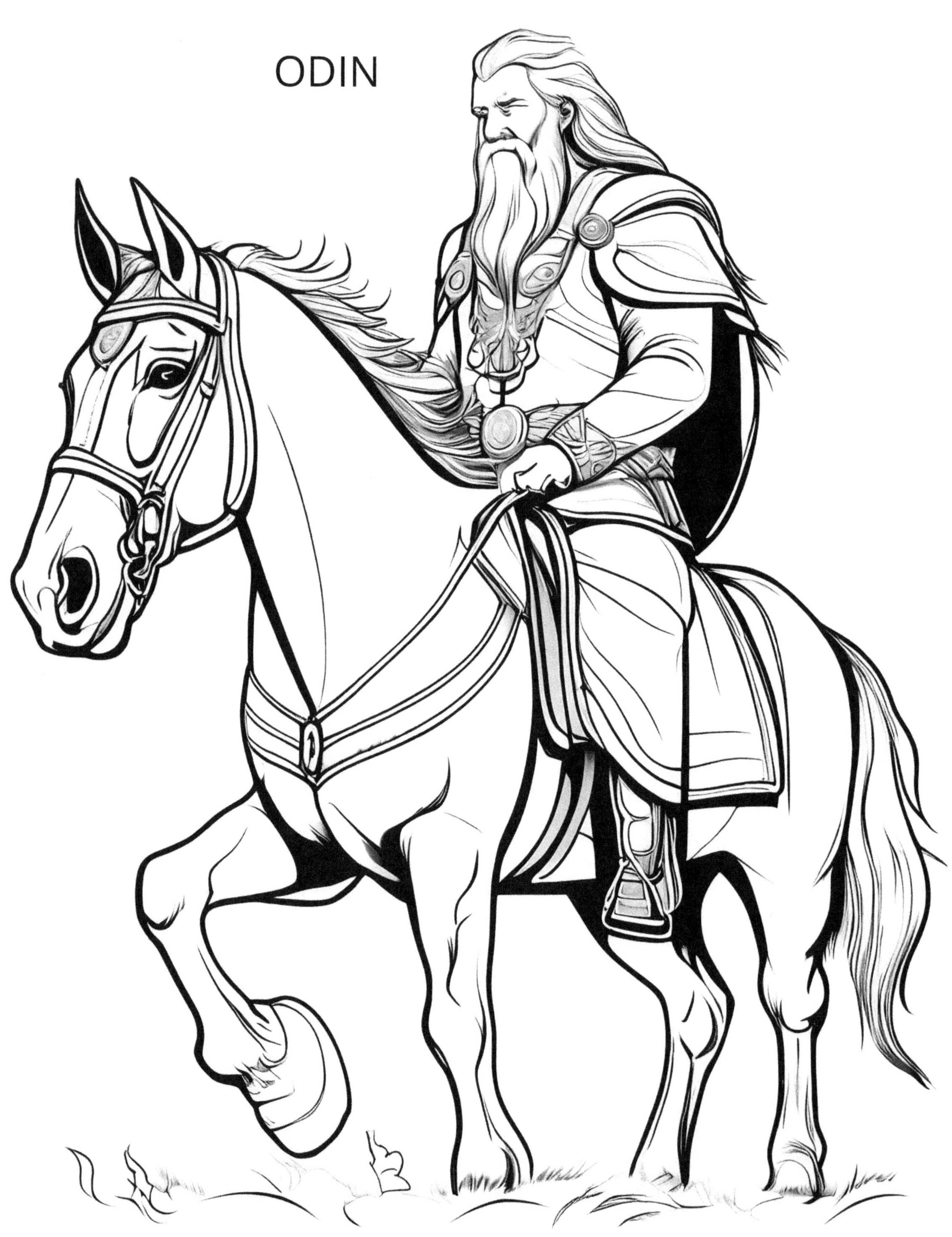

THOR

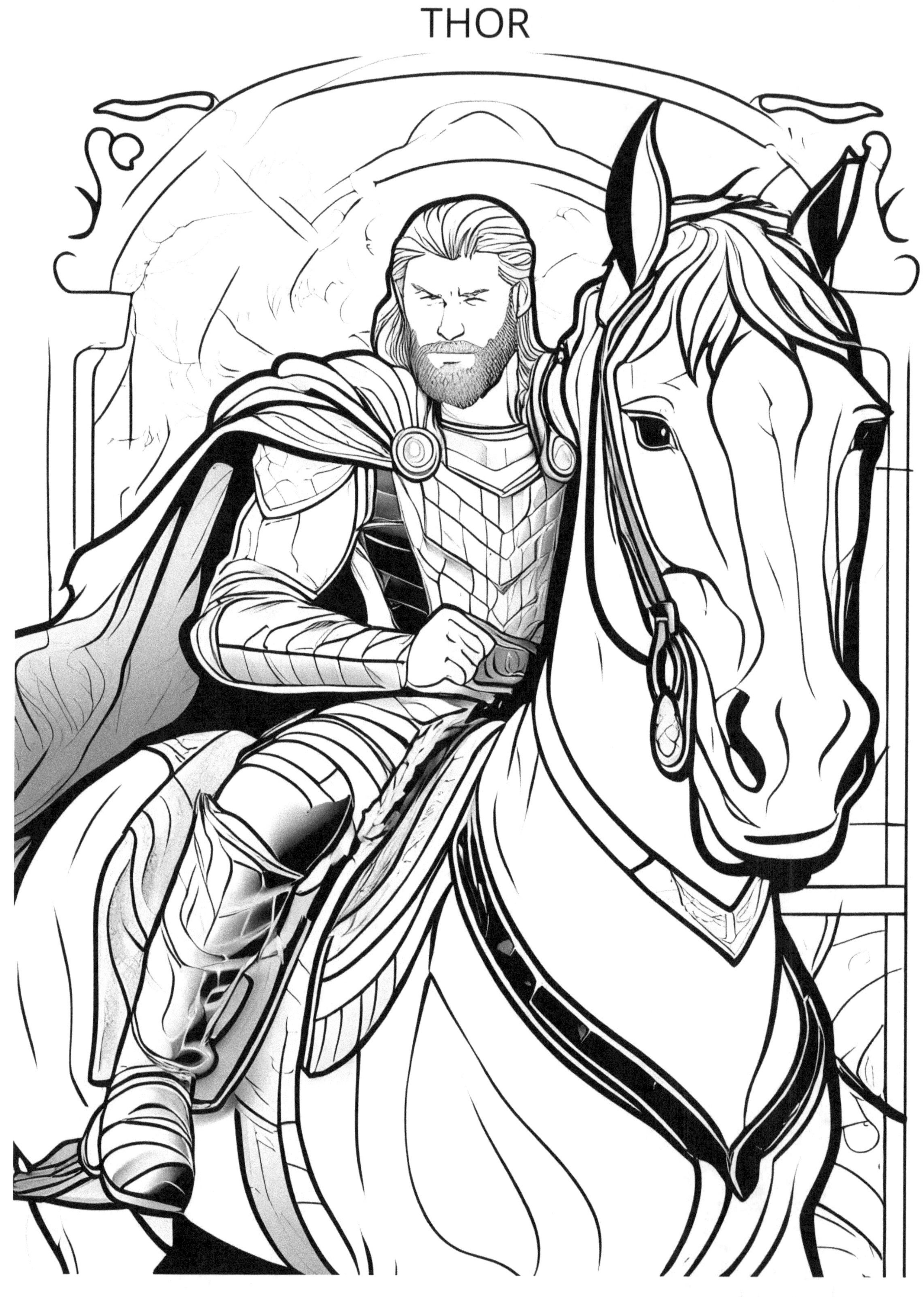

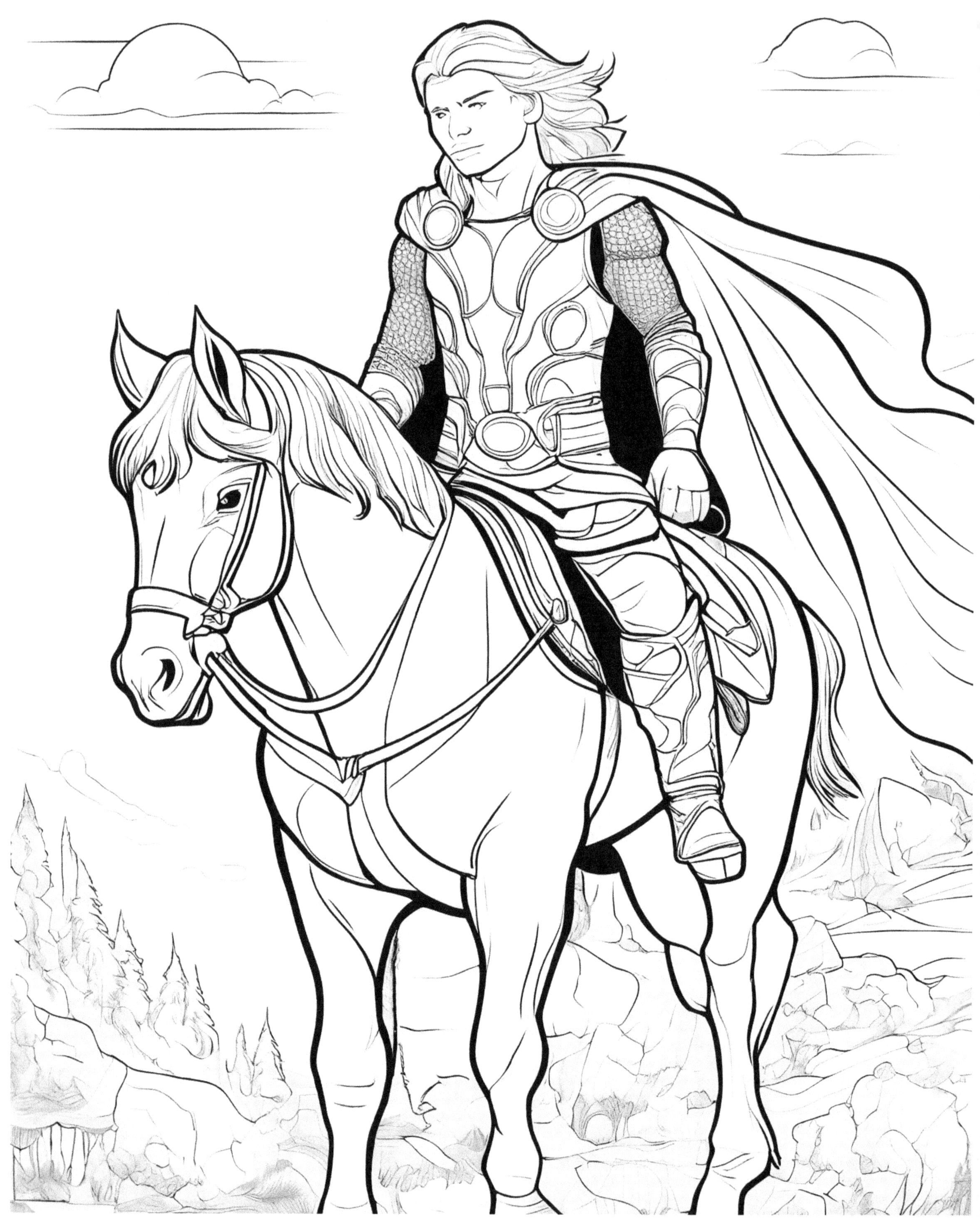

LOKI

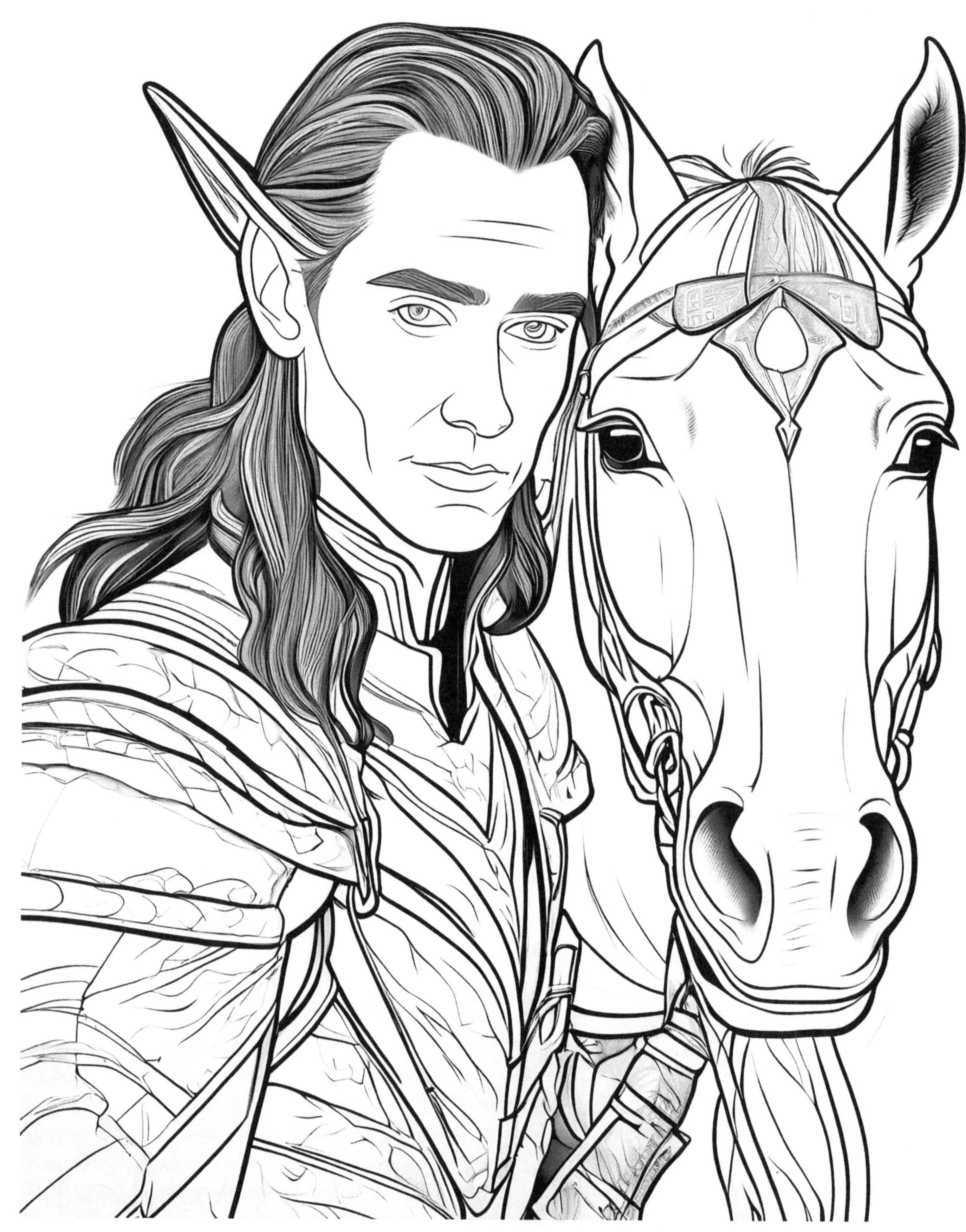

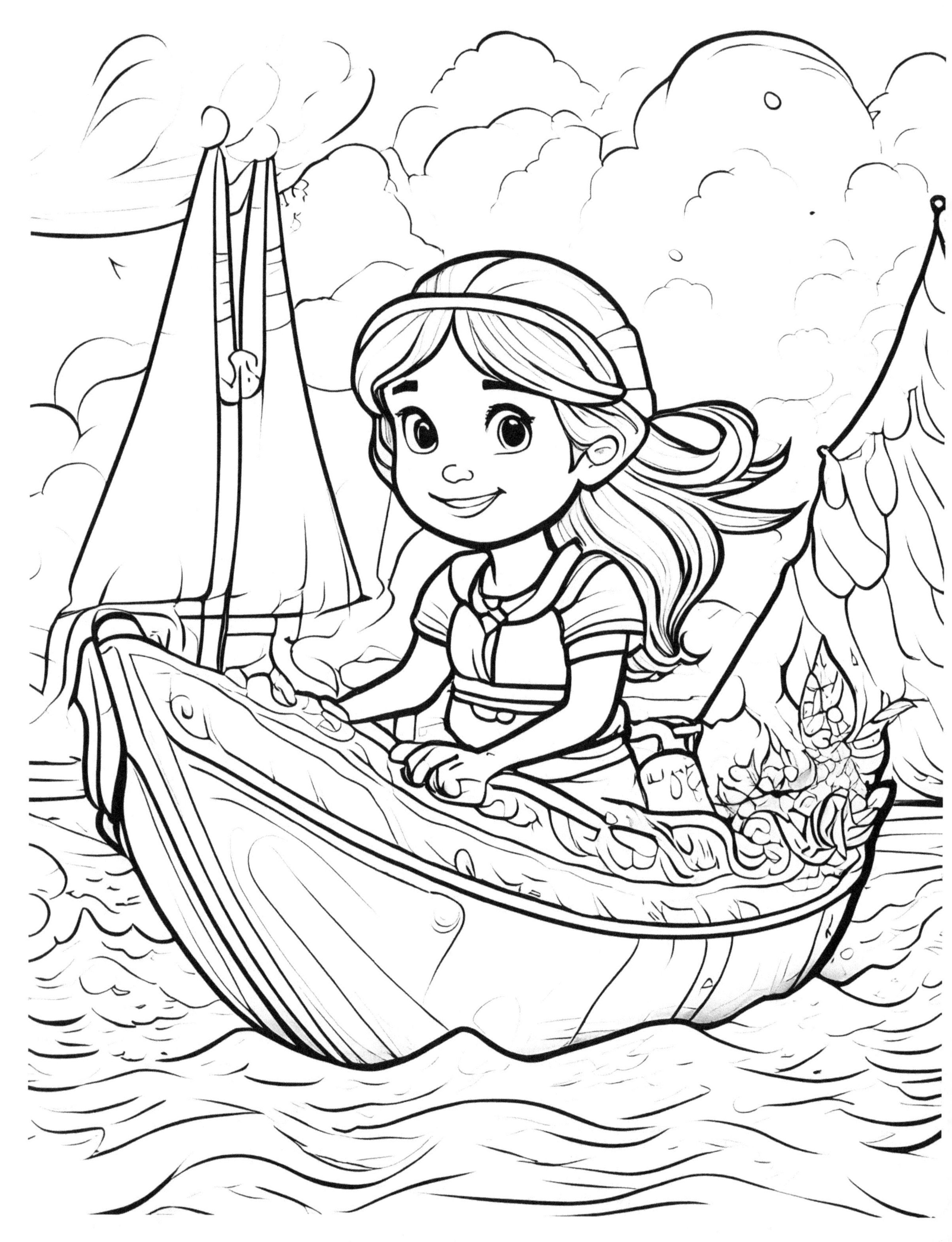

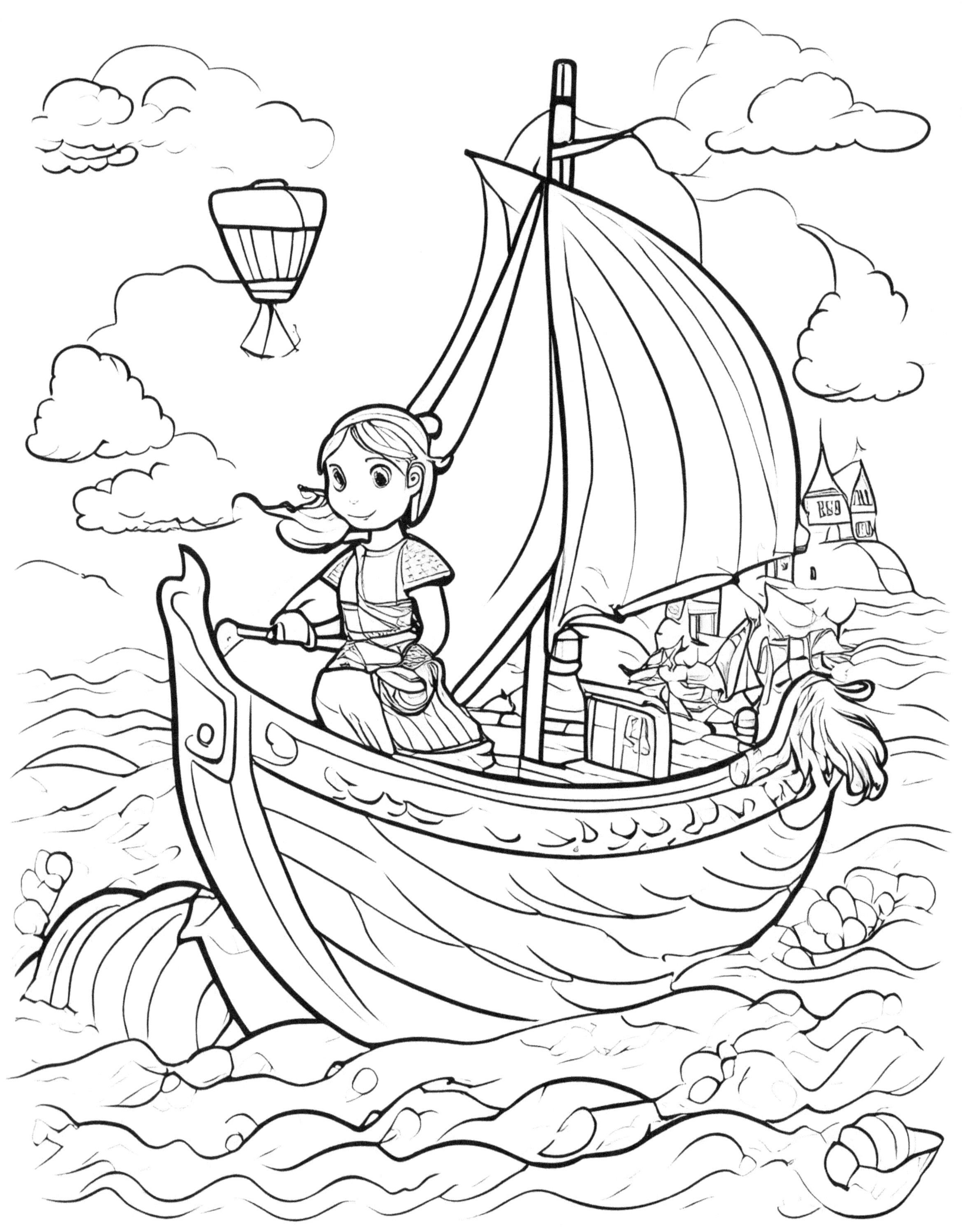

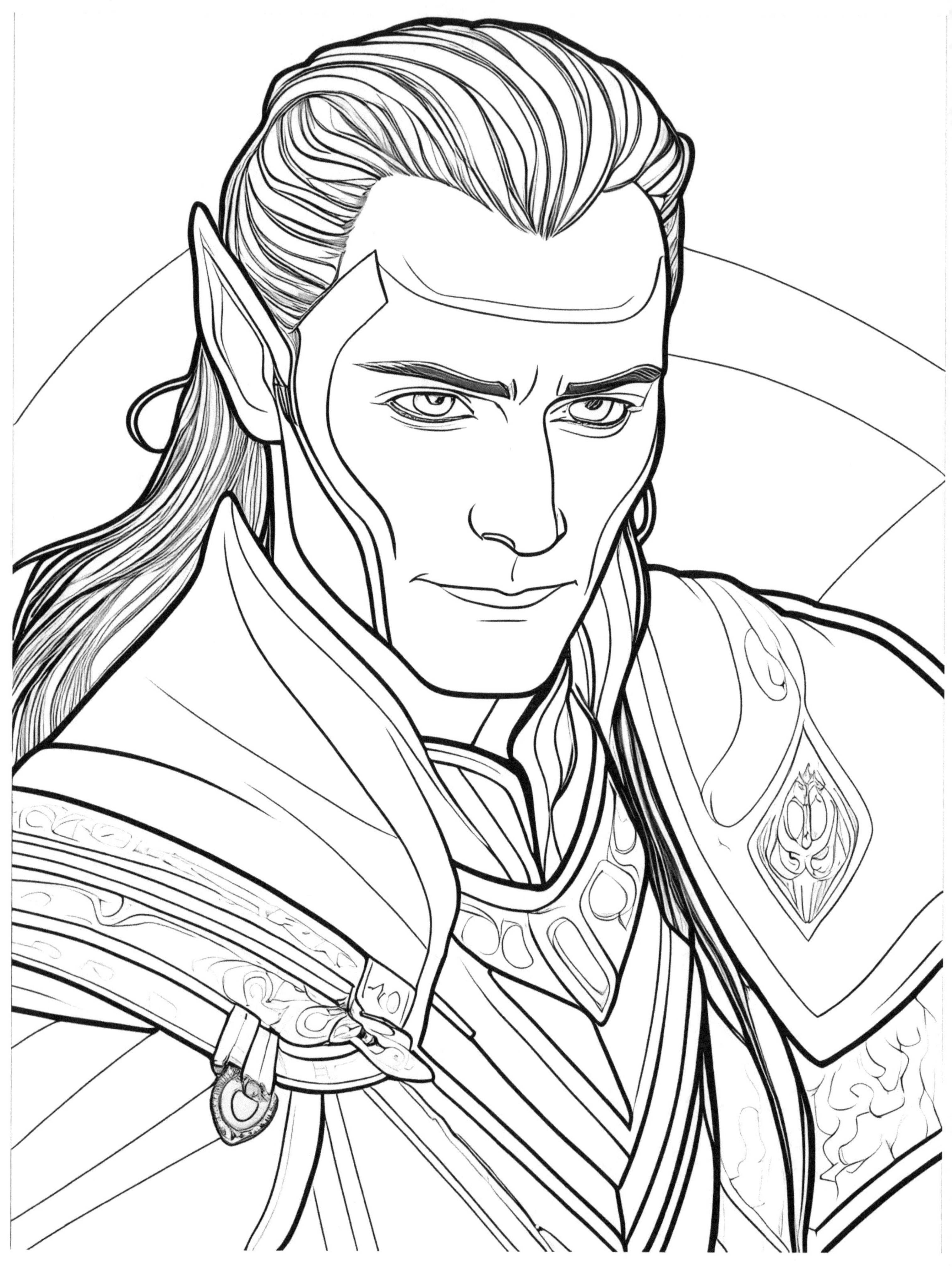

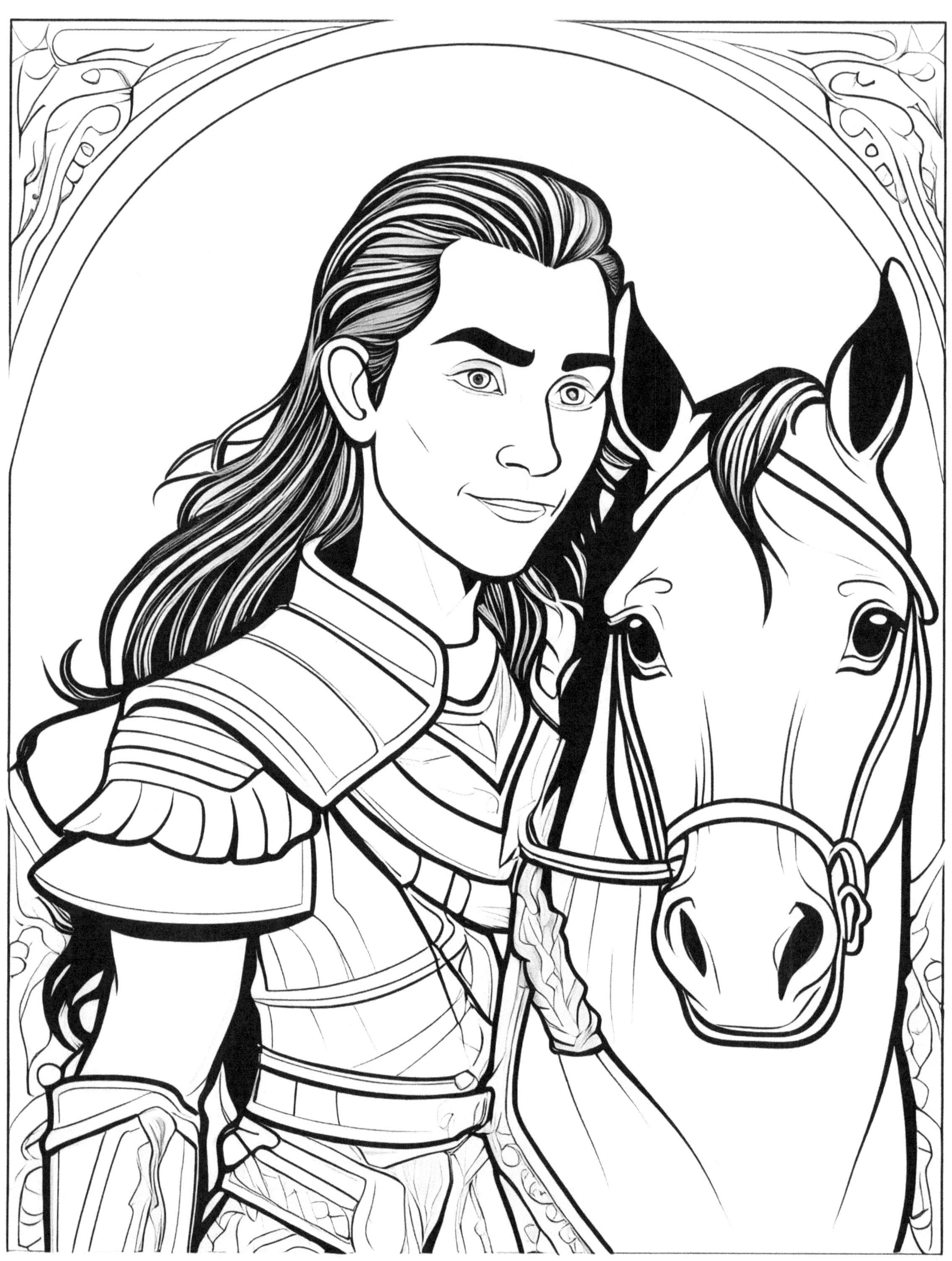

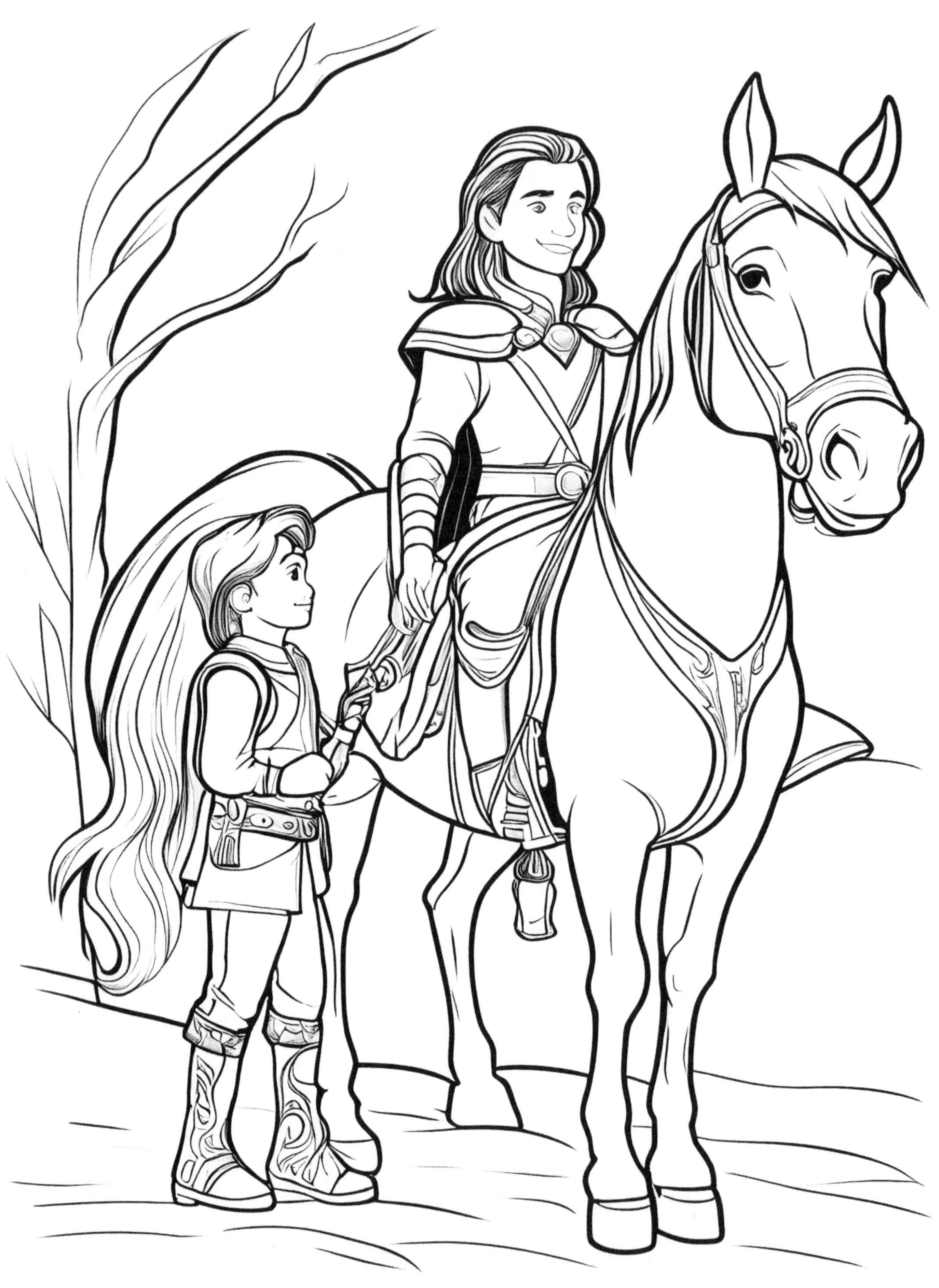

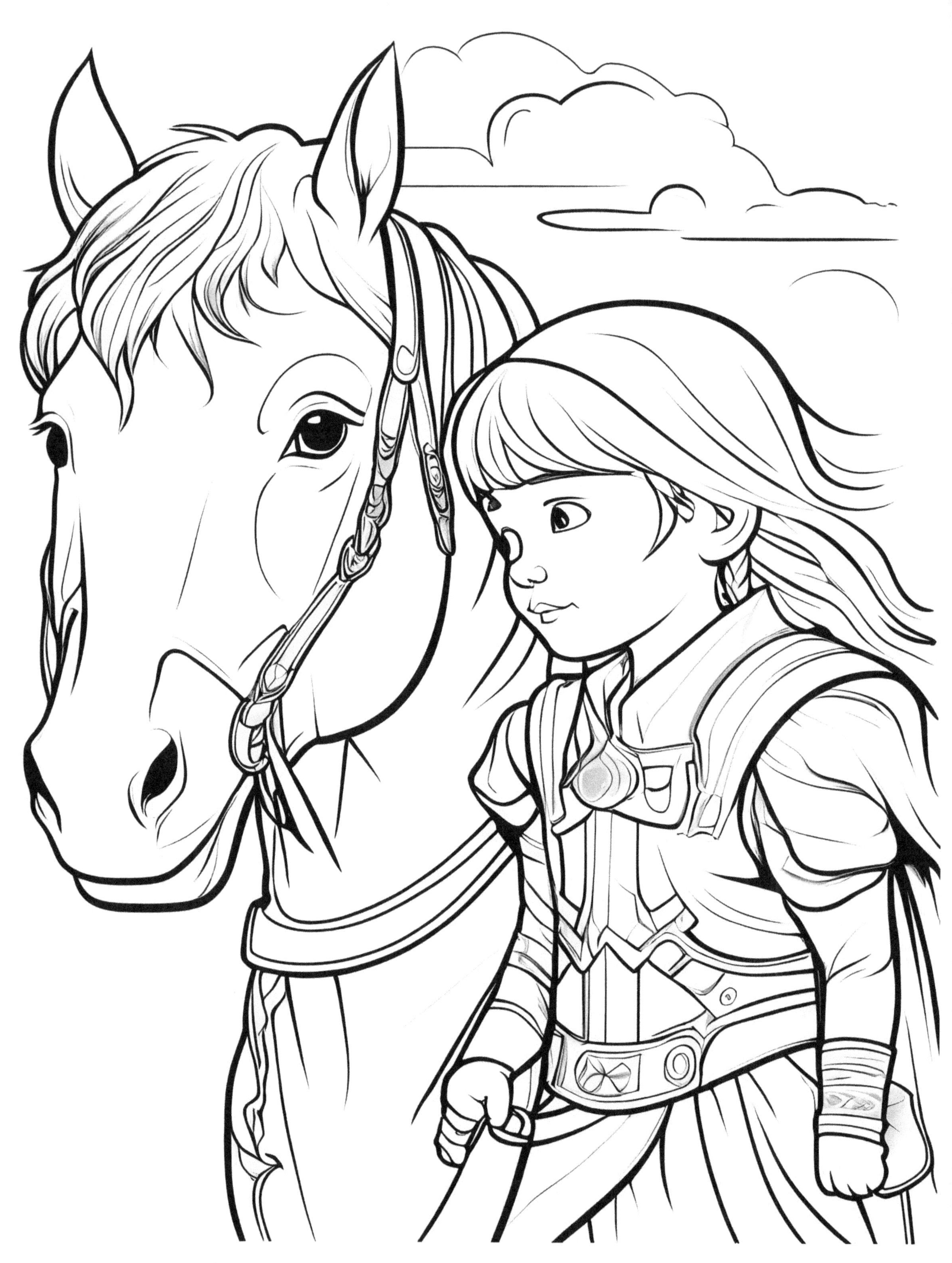

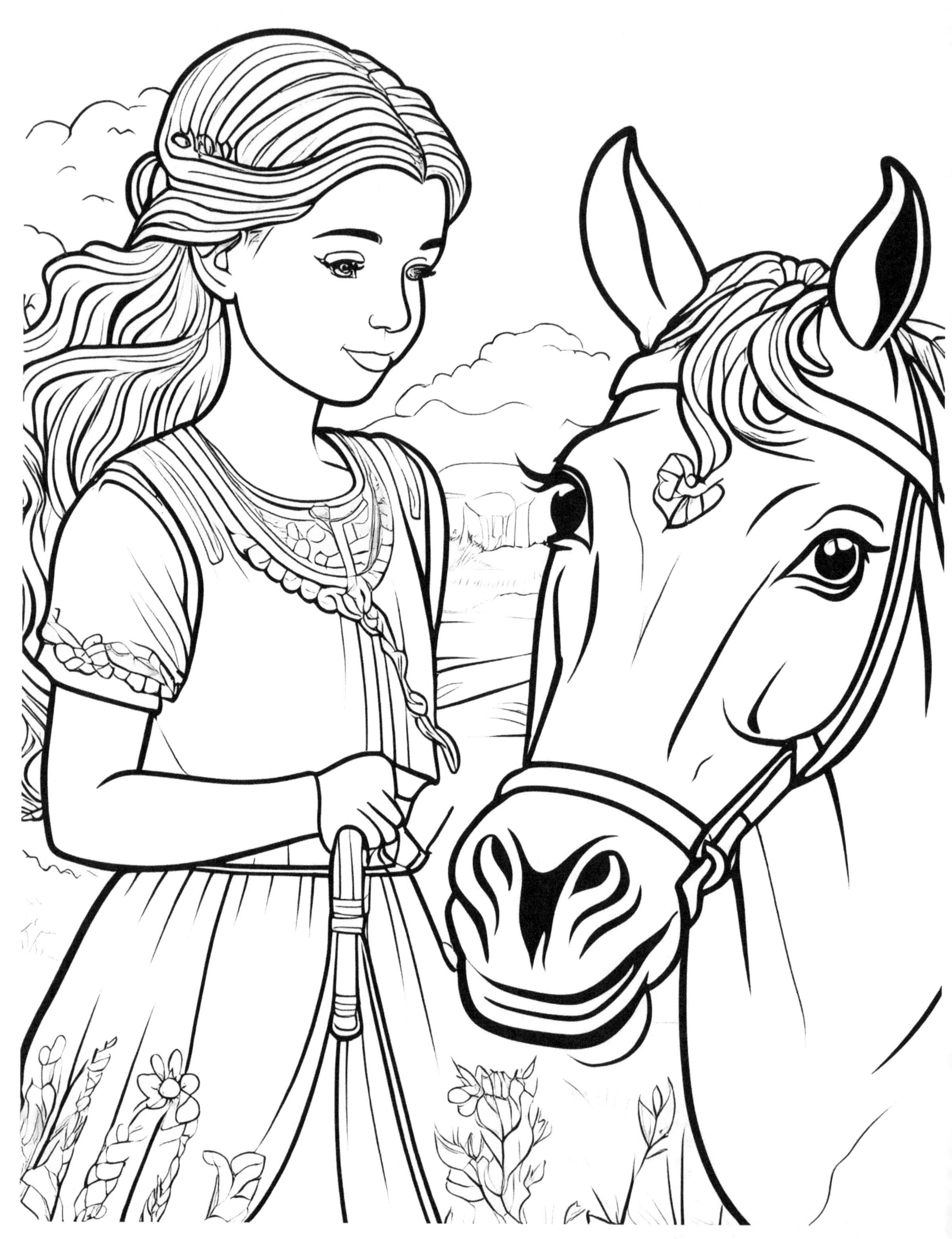

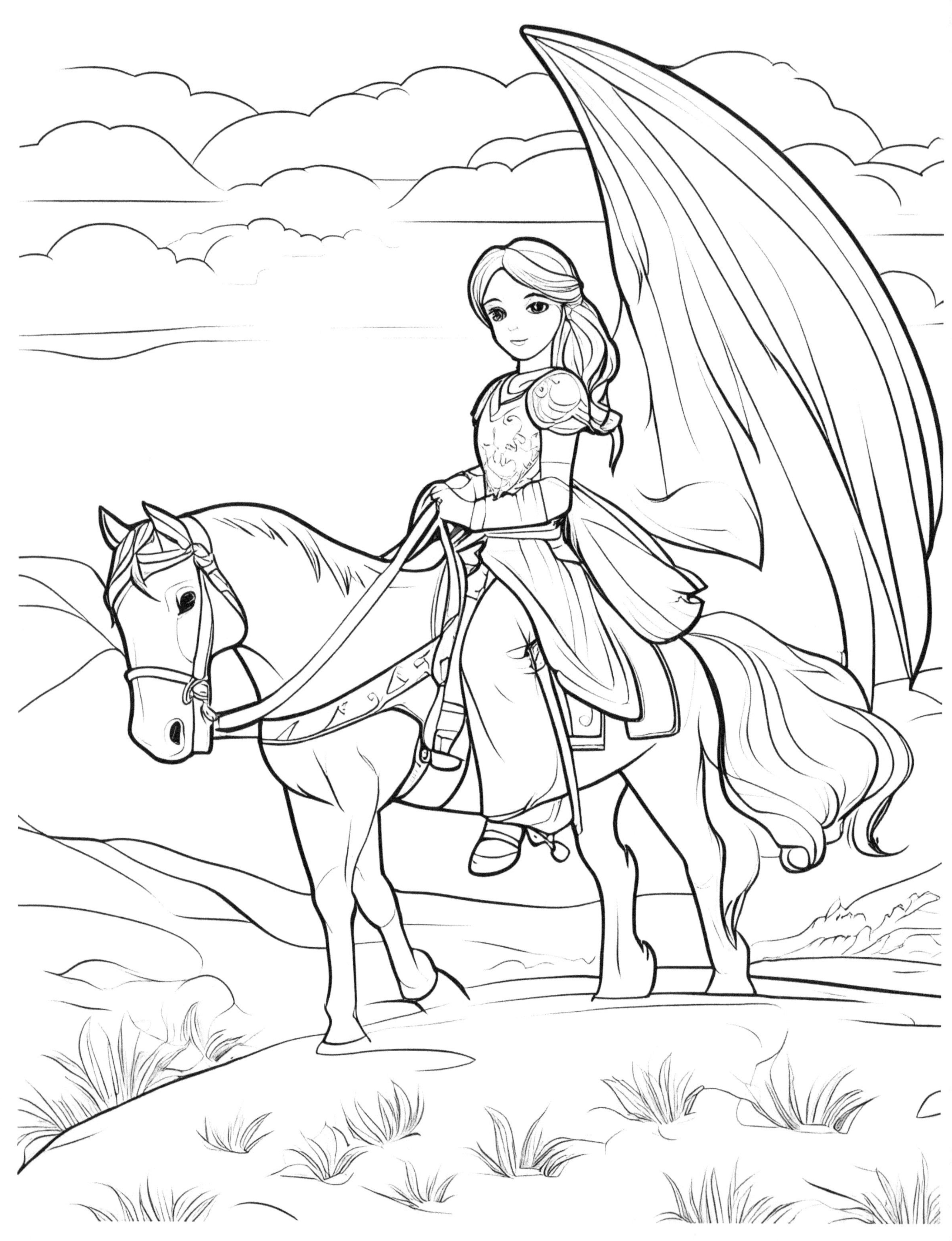

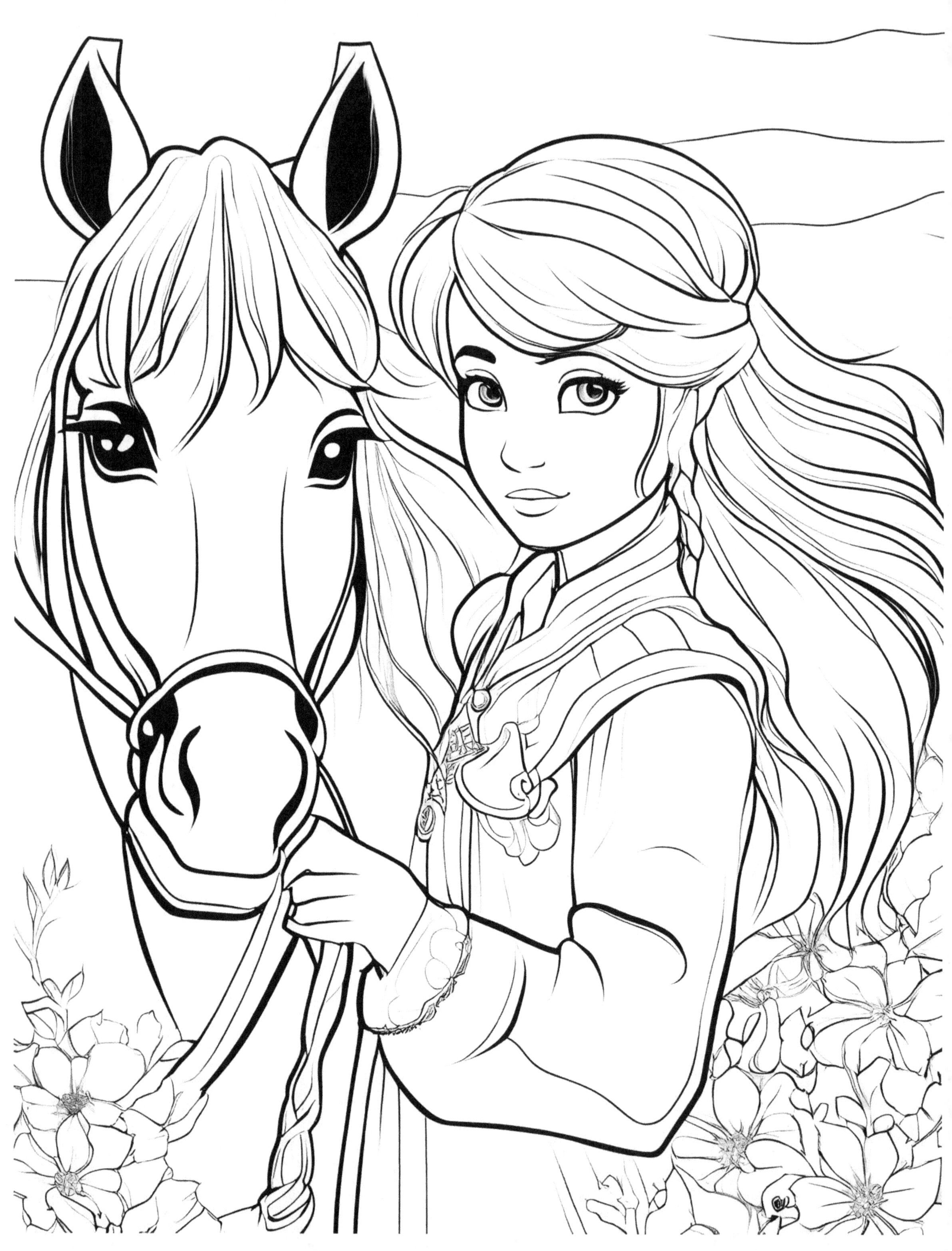